# Designing and Applying Experiential Learning in Higher Education

This insightful text is aimed specifically at educationalists and Higher Education lecturers who wish to adopt a more balanced, holistic, and inclusive approach to designing learning experiences. As lecturers are urged to adopt research-based teaching, it recognises the complexity of student learning and explains how knowledge can be constructed in various ways, not just socially and culturally, but also, for example, psychologically, emotionally, sensorially, biologically, and cognitively. The content covers design structures and formats that harness student capacities for learning, practical examples illustrating the core design principles for learning, and integrative designs for learning, well-being, and transformation. It provides a reflective space for readers to develop their teaching practice and expand their skills to embrace inclusive learning design to positively impact student engagement, understanding, and memory retention.

The *Critical Practice in Higher Education* series provides a scholarly and practical entry point for academics into key areas of Higher Education practice. Each book in the series explores an individual topic in depth, providing an overview in relation to current thinking and practice, informed by recent research. The series will be of interest to those engaged in the study of Higher Education, those involved in leading learning and teaching or working in academic development, and individuals seeking to explore particular topics of professional interest. Through critical engagement, this series aims to promote an expanded notion of being an academic – connecting research, teaching, scholarship, community engagement, and leadership – while developing confidence and authority.

**Colin Beard** is a Professor of Experiential Learning at Sheffield Hallam University in the UK. He is a National Teaching Fellow, and has held visiting professor roles in the UK, China, and Hong Kong. He has a wide experience base around experiential learning, spanning over 40 years in facilitating, training, teaching, and lecturing. He has worked with many universities and colleges around the globe delivering staff development programmes, and has been involved in learning design with government ministries, including ministries of education, and ministries concerned with ambassador and diplomat training. His experience also includes many leading corporate organisations, and charitable bodies. He is the co-founder of the Experiential Learning Design Institute, based in Hong Kong.

# Critical Practice in Higher Education

*Series editors: Joy Jarvis and Karen Mpamhanga*

This impactful series provides academics with a scholarly gateway into essential aspects of higher education practice. Perfect for those engaged in HE study, educational leadership roles, academic staff or anyone seeking to explore particular topics of interest. Delve into each text as it explores individual topics in depth connecting research, teaching, community engagement and leadership while developing confidence and authority.

**Critical Approaches to Online Learning**

*Julian McDougall*

**Bias-aware Teaching, Learning and Assessment**

*Donna Hurford and Andrew Read*

**Transition into Higher Education**

*Harriet Jones, Hilary Orpin, Gemma Mansi, Catherine Molesworth and Heather Monsey*

**Evidencing Teaching Achievements**

*Marita Grimwood and Steve McHanwell*

**Universal Design for Learning**

A Critical Approach

*Nicola Martin, Mike Wray and Joanna Krupa*

**Indicators of Teaching Excellence in Higher Education**

A Critical Approach

*Aneta Hayes and Nicholas Garnett*

**Designing and Applying Experiential Learning in Higher Education**

*Colin Beard*

For more information about this series, please visit: https://www.routledge.com/Critical-Practice-in-Higher-Education/book-series/CRITCPHE

# Designing and Applying Experiential Learning
## in Higher Education

**Colin Beard**

*Series Editors: Joy Jarvis and Karen Mpamhanga*

**CRITICAL PRACTICE IN HIGHER EDUCATION**

LONDON AND NEW YORK

Designed cover image: Adobe Stock

First published 2026
by Routledge
4 Park Square, Milton Park, Abingdon, Oxon OX14 4RN

and by Routledge
605 Third Avenue, New York, NY 10158

*Routledge is an imprint of the Taylor & Francis Group, an informa business*

© 2026 Colin Beard

The right of Colin Beard to be identified as author of this work has been asserted in accordance with sections 77 and 78 of the Copyright, Designs and Patents Act 1988.

All rights reserved. No part of this book may be reprinted or reproduced or utilised in any form or by any electronic, mechanical, or other means, now known or hereafter invented, including photocopying and recording, or in any information storage or retrieval system, without permission in writing from the publishers.

For Product Safety Concerns and Information please contact our EU representative GPSR@taylorandfrancis.com. Taylor & Francis Verlag GmbH, Kaufingerstraße 24, 80331 München, Germany.

*Trademark notice*: Product or corporate names may be trademarks or registered trademarks, and are used only for identification and explanation without intent to infringe.

*British Library Cataloguing-in-Publication Data*
A catalogue record for this book is available from the British Library

ISBN: 9781041211167 (hbk)
ISBN: 9781916925694 (pbk)
ISBN: 9781041054917 (ebk)

DOI: 10.4324/9781041054917

Typeset in Cambria
by codeMantra

This book is dedicated to my lovely wife Maggie, a committed and skilled teacher.

# Contents

| | | |
|---|---|---|
| | *List of figures* | *viii* |
| | *Meet the author and series editors* | *ix* |
| | *Acknowledgements* | *x* |
| Chapter 1 | An introduction to experiential learning design | 1 |
| Chapter 2 | A short history of experiential learning | 13 |
| Chapter 3 | Designs that utilise the core student capacities for learning | 28 |
| Chapter 4 | Experiential learning design and creative practice | 47 |
| Chapter 5 | Complex designs for experiential learning | 60 |
| Chapter 6 | Learning experience designs to enhance well-*being* | 68 |
| Chapter 7 | Final thoughts | 82 |
| | *References* | *84* |
| | *Index* | *89* |

# List of figures

| | | |
|---|---|---|
| 2.1 | The Holistic Experiential Learning Theory: seven capacities for learning | 25 |
| 3.1 | Three basic design structures | 30 |
| 3.2 | Design zone: illustrative contents | 32 |
| 3.3 | An illustrative route map design | 33 |
| 3.4 | Student engagement and the design of seminar route maps with descriptive text and depictive icons to enhance visual memory triggers | 34 |
| 3.5 | The learning combination lock | 36 |
| 3.6 | Moving to increased complexity: a visual representation | 39 |
| 4.1 | Summary of 12 core design principles | 48 |
| 6.1 | Balance and integration in the Holistic Experiential Learning Theory (HELT) model | 77 |

# Meet the **author and series editors**

**Colin Beard** is Professor Emeritus of Experiential Learning at Sheffield Hallam University. He is an innovative thinker and writer, globally recognised as leading the way with new theories of, and practical approaches to, experiential learning in the 21st century. With a Higher Education teaching experience spanning nearly 40 years, he was awarded a National Teaching Fellowship in 2005. An exceptional practitioner, his experience spans individual and organisational development work with medical educators, leading global corporates, NGOs, governments, and over 100 Higher and Further Education institutions. He has produced nearly 50 research papers, given 80 international keynotes, and written 10 books. He is the owner of Experience – the difference, consulting, and Founder and joint owner of the Experiential Learning Design Institute (ELDI), based in Hong Kong.

**Joy Jarvis** is currently Professor of Educational Practice at the University of Hertfordshire and a UK National Teaching Fellow. She has experience in a wide range of education contexts and works to create effective learning experiences for students and colleagues. She is particularly interested in the professional learning of those engaged in educational practice in Higher Education settings and has undertaken a range of projects, working with colleagues locally, nationally, and internationally to develop practice in teaching and leadership of teaching.

**Karen Mpamhanga** (formerly Karen Smith) is Professor of Higher Education and Professional Learning in the School of Education at the University of Hertfordshire. Her research focuses on how Higher Education policies and practices impact on those who work and study within universities. Karen has worked within educational development and on lecturer development programmes. She holds a Principal Fellowship of the Higher Education Academy and is cohort lead and supervisor on the University of Hertfordshire's Professional Doctorate in Education.

# Acknowledgements

I would like to acknowledge the support, advice, and encouragement that I have received from Professor Karen Mpamhanga and Professor Joy Jarvis during my journey. Thank you both for taking the time to understand my thinking and writing.

# Chapter 1 | An introduction to experiential learning design

# Introduction

This book offers Higher Education professionals the opportunity to reconsider and rethink the way that the student experience of learning is designed and delivered at a time when there have been substantial multi-disciplinary advancements in the learning sciences. The book is relatively short to make it accessible for busy professionals. Suggestions for further reading have been included at the end of each chapter.

Interest in experiential learning, where the central focus is on the 'experience' of learning, is once again gaining momentum across the globe. Experiential learning has developed so that new advanced design theories, practical tools, and models are more appropriate to learning in the 21st century. This book not only provides these new advanced design tools and theories, it also makes the case for learning in Higher Education to be experientially (pedagogically) inclusive, and holistic to support learner diversity. When conceived in a holistic way, learning is understood as utilising the core human capacities to experience the world, in embodied, embedded, enacted, relational, and extended ways (these terms are explored later). Learning is thus understood as not only socially and culturally 'constructed', but also psychologically, emotionally, sensorially, bodily, and cognitively constructed. As part of these 21st century advancements, a new Holistic Experiential Learning Theory (Beard, 2023) is presented in chapter 2 to highlight the way that 'experience' is the grounding source of learning.

My core strapline for student learning in Higher Education is: 'Let the Learners Experience the Learning'. So if we are not going to do the teaching and telling, then what needs to happen? Essentially I am suggesting less time spent on the design of talking and telling and showing slides, which tends to induce passivity. If you are not familiar with experiential learning I usually say 'Let the Learners *do* the Learning', as 'learning by doing' may be a more familiar phrase. However, when we say 'learning by doing' it adds to a common misconception of experiential learning. Experiential learning is not learning by 'doing' as it could simply mean doing anything! The word 'doing' needs to be critically unpacked, especially as the word suggests that experiential learning is simply being 'active', but what do we mean by active? Active intellectually, emotionally, socially, physically, bodily, sensorially? Across many parts of the globe this has been interpreted as physically active, resulting in experiential learning being regarded as only concerned with outdoor learning or adventure learning. The word activity does rightly suggest that movement is significant to learning, but the terms active, doing, movement, experience, and learning, and their role in experiential learning, require further critical scrutiny. That scrutiny will unfold in this and subsequent chapters. This book will bring readers up to date with contemporary thinking about experiential learning and its applications in Higher Education. Each chapter contains practical examples to illustrate potential ways forward, critical questions for practice to aid reflection and review, chapter summaries to reinforce the main messages, and recommended further reading to support further investigation. The book can be read by dipping into specific chapters to suit requirements, though it has been written so that the depth of understanding of experiential learning can be constructed chapter by chapter.

By substituting 'doing' with the more appropriate term of 'experience' there is greater alignment with 'experiential' learning. The strapline 'Let the Learners Experience the Learning' clearly suggests that experiential learning is both a design-focused and student-centred pedagogic approach. One interesting book title *Teaching With Your Mouth Shut* suggests that teachers should do less talking (Finkel, 2000). Though teaching with your mouth shut is not a realistic suggestion, Finkel considers that telling is essentially a 'default strategy' for many teachers, resulting in lost student potential. Teaching is no longer about the transmission of knowledge, though teachers in Higher Education often rely on specific descriptive (speech) and depictive formats (showing many visual images as 'slides' which students refer to as 'Death by PowerPoint', which is actually sensory habituation).

Transforming ways of 'teaching' is not easy: there is much to learn about how we humans experience the world and how we learn from our experiences. With good design the experience of learning takes centre-stage, encouraging students to become curious, more engaged, and more inquiring when 'acquainted with' aspects of their studies. A deeper understanding of the way humans experience the world will give a better understanding of human learning. If the experience of learning is special, as it is in 'experiential' learning, then it follows that there should be a much greater focus on experience design. Unpacking these terms, 'experience' and 'learning', is an important focus in this book.

## Critical question for practice

Do you consider that all teachers are 'designers' or 'architects' of student learning experiences?

Everyone involved in education is, arguably, an architect of learning design: that is what we do, but design time is often limited, or neglected. In teacher development programmes design processes are often simplified, despite learning design being a topic that has more recently gained considerable momentum: over a dozen books on learning experience design have been published early in the 21st century, and they herald important pedagogic changes. The following three titles are merely illustrative bugles of pedagogic change: *Teaching as a Design Science: Building Pedagogical Patterns for Learning and Technology* (Laurillard, 2012); *Higher Education by Design: Best Practices for Curricular Planning and Instruction* (Mackh, 2018); and *Experiential Learning Design: Theoretical Foundations and Effective Principles* (Beard, 2023). Despite the emergence of new design literature, the ability to design effective student experiences *for* and *of* learning is not easy: few of the design books attend to the sophistication inherent in the design of student learning.

# What do we mean by a learning experience?

As Maxine Sheets-Johnstone notes in *The Primacy of Movement* (2011), Western society not only has a tendency to be mesmerised by brains, it seems we have lost touch with our 'natural history'. Over many thousands of years humans have developed remarkable capacities for learning (for a concise chart see Beard, 2023).

New research on human learning is moving learning into the mid-21st century, though the understanding of learning lacks multi-disciplinary sophistication, neglecting some important student capacities to learn, and the consequence is unfulfilled potential. Pedagogic inclusivity requires that the full range of student capacities to learn should be considered in learning design. The argument presented in this book is that the student learning experience should be more integrated, and more comprehensively holistic.

All learning experiences are embodied (the mind relies on body-based intelligence) and embedded (interactions with the external environment). The inner world of learning is an embodied experience that is mostly private. The outer world experience is one that students are embedded in: and this world is where teachers have slightly more control and influence. Learning is also relational (involving social interaction), enacted (agency/put into practice/behaviours), and extended (specific tools and objects for example enhance learning and become extensions of brain-body capacities). These concepts underscore the inherently complex and sophisticated nature of human learning, and we as teachers have to understand and embrace this sophistication and the multiple realities of the 21st century rather than seeing learning as a straightforward, ordered process.

But there is a problem with complexity as will be further highlighted in chapter 2: without order, complexity confuses, and so there is a need to find a balance between simplicity and complexity (see Van Geert and Wagemans, 2020). To this end a new Holistic Experiential Learning Theory (HELT), suitable for design in the 21st century, is introduced in the next chapter, as a model that embraces sophistication, whilst, hopefully, being elegantly simple, ordered, and memorable. The HELT modelling is the result of a consilience, a term that signifies that a considerable body of multi-disciplinary research has identified common findings that identify several core capacities available to humans for the purpose of learning. If learning is perceived as a relatively simple process, pedagogic diversity will continue to be neglected. Back in 1938, in *Experience and Education*, Dewey called for a philosophy of experience. So, what might this philosophy of experience look like?

Experiences create neural 'pathways', and these pathways are responsible for memory. Memories naturally fade, and many memories become reconfigured, or distorted, in the processes of building on previous experiences. These neural 'pathways' require frequent use to prevent decline. We say: 'use it or lose it'! Well-known research by Maguire and her colleagues explored why London taxi drivers had an enlarged part of their hippocampus, an area of the brain responsible for memory and spatial cognition (Maguire et al., 2000): she also discovered how this area reduced after retirement. Research shows that when the hippocampus is damaged or has decay, as in dementia, then memories of space are affected. Rather interestingly, the *'motivation behind this study was, in part, the finding that the hippocampus is larger in birds that store food in different locations than those that do not'* (Dudchenko, 2010, p 186).

## Example 1.1

### Why did I come here?

Have you ever gone into another room only to forget why you went there? Then, when you head back to where you came from you remember! This association of space with memory is very significant for learning. Let me illustrate this with reference to a specific event when I was working with NHS senior managers. We did a quick review of the day, like a mental video playback, but no one could remember what happened after lunch. There was a long pause. Then someone said: 'we were over there in a circle'. The reference to space was sufficient to release the memory of what we were doing, and this release occurred almost simultaneously in all of us when reference was made to where we did what we did.

Neuroscience research is opening-up new thinking about the human brain and the term neuro*diversity* has now become popular. Yet it is not only the human brain that is diverse: the nervous system spreads out into the human body, a body which is equally diverse, and equally capable of learning. Our sensory capacities are diverse, as are our feelings, as well as the social and cultural relationships that we experience. Diversity is wide-ranging: an inclusive pedagogy recognises that learning occurs in a complex state of flux, connecting, to differing extents, these diverse capacities.

On the first page of chapter 1 of *Experience and Education*, Dewey says '*Mankind likes to think in terms of extreme opposites. It is given to formulating beliefs in terms of Either-Ors, between which it recognizes no intermediate possibilities*' (1938, p 17). Dewey then states that '*The history of educational theory is marked by opposition between the idea that education is development from within, and that it is formation from without*' (1938, p 17). Oppositional thinking, recognised as problematic by Dewey, is challenged in this book; the symbol ~ creates the notion of complimentary pairs, rather than polar opposites: ~ represents 'everything in-between' and Kelso and Engstrom (2006) have devoted a whole book to this divisive issue.

# Redesigning design

Our job as teachers is certainly complex, and this is reflected by just two words that are difficult to define: learning and experience. The meaning of these words has been hotly debated by philosophers for centuries. After 50 years of working in training, facilitation, and teaching with a variety of global institutions, I have come to realise that Higher Education institutions are particularly good at planning and management, at developing rules, structures, and policies, and creating measures and controls for calculating 'performance'. Within this tradition, the teaching design focuses on documentation referred to as a lesson plan, as part of a planning process. Objectives and outcomes generate a degree of predictability, whereas choreography recognises the complex flux, the dance of learning where unpredictability abounds. For teachers this means there is always an element of risk in the improvisation of teaching.

*In an age preoccupied by outcomes, the processes of experiential learning are often seen to be of subsidiary interest. As a result, a theory of experiential learning, which focuses principally on processes rather than outcomes, runs against the current tide of fascination for competence, performance, and anything that can be tightly linked to the products of learning.*

(Stein, 2004, p 19)

Significant numbers of students fail to attend seminars and lectures, and this worrying trend is being addressed by institutions tightening up on attendance monitoring. This approach may fail to address the real underlying issues about the teaching experience.

# Do pedagogically inclusive designs have a greater impact on student learning?

Lecturers are urged to deliver 'research-informed teaching', however, as Catherine Bovill points out, many colleagues know about research in specialist subjects, but they are likely to be less knowledgeable about research on learning and teaching (2020). Lack of in-depth knowledge about the role that experience plays in Higher Education learning (*for* and *of* learning), and 'research-informed teaching' being interpreted as research-informed subject matter, all contribute to an imperative for a new approach to the design of the student experience of learning.

Whilst learning design is complex, there are important 'universals' operating that can be utilised for experiential design. Lakoff and Nunez suggest that it is now widely accepted that much of the brain is devoted to *'vision, motion, spatial understanding, interpersonal interaction, coordination, emotions, and language'* (2000, p 1). The structure of the brain appears to 'reflect' these universals of learning design. If we examine emerging pedagogies in Higher Education, they too mirror, or 'reflect', these universal capacities for learning. Relational pedagogy, for example, focuses on the social and interpersonal interactions (see Gravett, 2024), as does *co-creation* (Bovill, 2020). The enhancement of sensory capacities in multi-media explores the body-brain partnership with sensory experiences (see Mayer, 2014). Spatial cognition (Gattis, 2001) is concerned with bodily capacities such as coordination, movement, and the embodied sense of space in the process of thinking (Macrine and Fugate, 2022). Object-based learning explores object manipulation by the body (Chatterjee and Hannan, 2016). Research on student emotions in Higher Education highlights how the emotions play a key role in the pleasure of learning (Beard et al., 2014; Clayton et al., 2009). Learning communities (see Wenger, 1998) enhance a student's sense of belonging (Baumeister and Leary, 1995). Research on extended learning explores how extensions to our bodily capacities (such as a pencil, computer, or AI) support and extend human learning (Clark, 2011). Multi-disciplinary, holistic design approaches to learning work with many of these human capacities for learning, and as new pedagogies continue to emerge, they collectively signpost an exciting future.

Students possess significant capacities to think (cognitive capacities), to do, and to act (conative capacities/agency), to sense (e.g. touch, feel, manipulate, and move) and give attentional focus (receptive–perceptive attentional capacities, multi-media), to have feelings (affective capacities), to belong (social and more than human interaction, attachment, and affiliation capacities), and to become and be someone (ontological capacities). Inclusive pedagogies hold real promise to engage a greater number of students using these core capacities to learn.

In example 1.2, the short and simple story about young children is introduced to highlight a range of universal learning and teaching principles.

## Example 1.2

### Contemporary approaches to mathematics teaching in young children

Imagine an infant holding the hands of their parents and walking up a set of stairs. The parents, in a rhythmic fashion, emphatically say: 1......2......3.......4 and so on. The parents are teaching the infant to count. However, what the parents often don't realise is that this 'experience' of counting is not simply rote or recital learning. The infant is using their body to move up the concrete objects (steps) to gain a conceptual understanding of numbers: step 6 for example is 'higher' than step 4. This concept is spatial: the infant gains a spatial-conceptual understanding of higher and lower numbers. This learning experience is also a social act in that parents are holding the hands of the infant and making the experience fun (affective, embodied capacities).

The infants eventually attend school where they are taught mathematics. The primary school teacher uses sweets to show the children the principle of 'sharing', which eventually becomes 'dividing'. Dividing eventually becomes a symbol, that can form part of an equation. The sweets are initially used as concrete objects, and the movement of the sweets by the children in the process of sharing (an everyday linguistic term) involves the body, particularly the dexterity of the infants' hands. Eventually the children understand the linguistic shift to a mathematical term, along with the symbolic form. Over time young children learn to carry out division without the body moving concrete objects. It is likely they will be able to imagine these spatial processes (experiences) that involved the body. The process of dividing is ultimately carried out solely in the head. Eventually, over time, mathematics becomes solely a cognitive process.

This simple story highlights some of the same core processes of *experiential* learning that are increasingly being utilised in 'higher' levels of education to scaffold cognitive processing, albeit in more complex form.

# Why is spatial cognition and movement so important to learning?

Living creatures are *animate*; they move, and if they move, they are alive. All animals move towards something, such as food, and away from preying creatures and danger. We also know that infants 'grasp' the world out there, literally and epistemologically through movement. Indeed, movement is said to be '*the generative source of our primal sense of aliveness and of our primal capacities for sense-making*' (Sheets-Johnstone, 2011, p 114; see also Sheets-Johnstone, 1990; Sheets-Johnstone, 2009). The term animation, used in multi-media, refers to movement (see Mayer, 2014), and an animateur, like teachers, is someone who leads and encourages participation in a particular activity. Proponents of embodied cognition suggest that our experience in space, and the cognitive structures we develop to perceive, navigate, and remember space, are the indispensable foundations of all complex abstract cognitive tasks (Gattis, 2001): '*Caught up in an adult world, we easily lose sight of movement and of our fundamental capacity to think in movement. Any time we care to turn our attention to it, however, there it is*' (Maxine Sheets-Johnstone, 2011, p 448).

# Is *experiential* learning gaining ground across the globe?

Experiential learning is deemed a theoretical position, a philosophy, and a practice. Experiential learning, as a genre of learning approaches, has a long and significant history based on concerns about the way that education and learning is experienced. New thinking in the 19th, 20th, and 21st centuries has resulted in experiential learning becoming more developed, and more complex, with a greater diversification of practice. Recent advances in knowledge about learning, particularly within neuroscience, have resulted in new developments within experiential learning in the 21st century (Beard, 2023). Experiential learning is undergoing a revival. In educational institutions across the globe people are being assigned role titles as experiential learning specialists in Higher Education Institutions (HEIs) and schools.

Experience and learning are two of the most complex words in any dictionary, much debated by ancient philosophers. Experience is a term historian Martin Jay suggests '*exceeds concepts and even language itself*' and that '*vicarious experience is not the real thing, which has to be directly undergone*' (2005, p 5). 'Experiential' learning is a type of learning where the focus is on the nature of the learner 'experience', where experience holds special status, taking centre-stage in design. Experiential learning, as a category or type of learning, implies that the nature of the 'experience' of learning has considerable significance. Experiential learning is also said to be one of four canonical approaches to adult learning, alongside andragogy, transformative learning, and self-directed learning (Belzer and Dashew, 2023).

Despite tentative claims by Seaman et al. (2017) that the term was first used in human relations training by Kurt Lewin in the USA, it appears that an 'experiential approach' was in common use, evolving naturally into experiential learning (see Boydell, 1976; Torbert, 1972). An early publication by Kolb et al., in 1971 was titled *Organizational Psychology: An Experiential Approach*; this term was frequently used in publications in the 1970s (Knudson et al., 1973; McLennan circa. 1974 in Boydell, 1976).

Despite being widely used in the 'experience economy' (Pine and Gilmore, 1999), the experiential learning literature lacks a critical examination of the term 'experience'. Although our core human genetic template presents a generic structure for the development of the brain, the detailed wiring is significantly sculpted by the way we experience the world. Experiences shape our becoming (becoming someone), and who we are or think we are (identity, values, beliefs, sense of self). We learn through and by experience, and experience changes the brain structure, resulting in neurodiversity. The sub-title of a book by child psychiatrist Daniel Siegel points to key experiential processes: it is called *The Developing Mind: How Relationships and the Brain Interact to Shape Who We Are* (2015).

Understanding how we experience the world may help create a more advanced definition of experiential learning. Essentially, we sense and perceive, we have feelings, we think and reflect, we do and act, we experience considerable social interaction, including attachments to people and places, and friendships create a sense of belonging. These capacities combine to create an integrated, unified experience.

## Critical question for practice

What is the difference between Experiential Education and Experiential Learning – or are they the same thing?

Although these terms are often used interchangeably, partly for historical reasons that will be exposed in the next chapter, perhaps the best way to answer this question is to consider that phylogenetically (in an evolutionary sense) and ontogenetically (in a developmental sense) learning precedes education. Interestingly it is transformation, in an ontological sense, that is said to be the fundamental concern of Higher Education: Barnett considers the wider project of Higher Education is not the development of the epistemological self, but rather the development of the ontological self (Barnett, 2007). The strapline at my university is 'We Transform Lives'.

## Attempts to define experiential learning

Perhaps the most well-known model of experiential learning is that of the experiential learning cycle by Kolb and Fry (1975). Kolb acknowledges that the learning cycle, commonly taught in teacher training, was in fact built on the reflective enquiry approach developed by Kurt Lewin when working on group development and social relations. Kolb also adapted earlier thinking about the 'scientific method' that was recommended for schools to adopt by John Dewey in the USA.

The learning cycle by Kolb suggests a stage approach to learning that in essence could be seen as a re-representation of the scientific method, consisting of hypothesising, experimenting, reflecting, and redesigning/changing. The experiential learning cycle similarly consists of having a concrete experience (equivalent to experimenting), followed by reflection so that new ideas or practices can be formulated. These are then followed up with practical testing. The term 'concrete experience' for Kolb and others involved the use of management 'games' and 'simulations' (see Kolb, 1973). Kolb states that *'learning is a process whereby knowledge is created through the transformation of experience'* (1984, p 38). Many years later, Itin (1999), an outdoor educator, moved from the philosophical to the practical in his definition of experiential 'education' as:

*a holistic philosophy, where carefully chosen experiences supported by reflection, critical analysis, and synthesis, are structured to require the learner to take initiative, make decisions, and be accountable for the results, through actively posing questions, investigating, experimenting, being curious, solving problems, assuming responsibility, being creative, constructing meaning, and integrating previously developed knowledge.*

(p 93)

Nearly 20 years later, myself and a colleague (Beard and Wilson, 2018) define 'experiential' learning as interactional, as holistic, harnessing many of the human capacities for learning:

*a sense making process involving significant experiences that, to varying degrees, act as the source of learning for individuals, groups, and organisations. These experiences actively immerse and reflectively engage the inner world of learner(s) as whole beings (including physical-bodily, intellectually, emotionally, psychologically, and spiritually) with the intricate 'outer world' of the learning environment, in places and spaces, within the social, cultural, and political milieu to create memorable, rich and effective experiences for, and of learning.*

(p 3)

The three definitions are all informative: together they move towards an increased sophistication in understanding the defining parameters of experiential learning.

# Improving the student learning experience

The five remaining chapters of this book will consider how we can improve the student learning experience, so that the students become more fully 'acquainted with', rather than merely 'gaining knowledge of', a topic or subject. Some of the fascinating topics included in the chapters to come are:

- Basic structural and choreographic design principles that support the design of any educational discipline.
- How experience can be harnessed as the foundation 'of' and 'for' learning.
- Designs that embrace neurodiversity, inclusivity, and 'whole'-person learning.
- Recent research findings concerning the significance of linguistics in design, including the impact of spatial metaphors for cognitive scaffolding.
- The concept of making learning and thinking visible, to avoid 'errors of imagination' inherent in transmission-based teaching methods.
- The design of a range of tools and materials that can be utilised as navigational (scaffolding) aids to support the deep learning and understanding of complex subjects.
- The design of co-production, co-creation, and inheritance to create positive learning habits.
- An introduction to important connections between mental health and well-being, and learning in Higher Education.

## Summary

- This broad-ranging introductory chapter sets the scene for a more detailed examination of the importance and impact of utilising holistic experiential learning designs in Higher Education. The term 'holistic', explored here in an introductory sense, is further examined in the coming chapters. The central argument presented here is that the full range of student capacities to learn are not being fully utilised.

- The chapter has also introduced the importance of identifying and understanding the core human capacities that are utilised in learning. These capacities have been honed through our extensive 'natural history'. This enlightening history will be further discussed and developed in chapter 2.

# Useful texts

Macrine, S and Fugate, J (2022) (eds) *Movement Matters: How Embodied Cognition Informs Teaching and Learning.* Cambridge, MA: MIT Press.

*This book focuses on the reasons why movement and embodied cognition are important to the understanding of teaching and learning.*

Beard, C and Wilson, J (2018) (4th edition) *Experiential Learning: A Practical Guide to Training, Coaching and Education.* London: Kogan Page.

*This book offers teachers, trainers, and facilitators a general introductory level to many, but not all, of the core issues that are highlighted in this book.*

# Chapter 2 | A short history of experiential learning

## Introduction

Many educators are unsure what experiential learning really is, and so to get a better understanding of what it was, how it evolved, and what it might become in the future, this chapter briefly looks back at its pre-historical and historical roots. By exploring the everyday challenges that hominids faced over many thousands of years, the early evolutionary developments that created the foundational capacities to learn are exposed.

Later, the main trajectories that appear to have led to the development of experiential learning during the 19th, 20th, and 21st centuries highlight a diverse multiplicity of meanings and practices, and also misunderstandings. Aspects of power, gender, politics, emancipation, and resistance to tradition are all exposed. What emerges is a deficiency in the principal narratives concerning the history of experiential learning. Many stories of the roots of experiential learning that go beyond dominant Western, mainly US interpretations, are yet to emerge. When these do surface, experiential learning will develop in new and rich directions, and experiential learning is likely to become more holistic, inclusive, and representative. An illustrative example of such an emerging story is found in the remarkable depth of learning and wisdom about sea navigation achieved through the inter and intra generational experience of Polynesian sailors (see Davis, 2009).

This chapter argues that the current understanding of experiential learning is overly simplistic in ways that have negatively influenced teaching practice. When critical commentaries about experiential learning from leading writers coalesce, what emerges is a common call for experiential learning to embrace wider, multi-disciplinary and trans-disciplinary perspectives.

# Pre-history and the development of human capacities to learn

If learning is that which is derived from and by experience, then from the natural history perspective it could be argued that experiential learning is all there ever was. With 3,500,000,000 years of adaptive processes, which have been foundational to the early development of significant human capacities to learn from experience, they continue to be refined and upgraded. So, what are these capacities for learning?

Because the body and brain have co-evolved to function as a partnership, much of the brain, as was noted in chapter 1, is devoted to seven major functions, notably *'vision, motion, spatial understanding, interpersonal interaction, coordination, emotions, and language'* (Lakoff and Nunez, 2000, p 1). This leads to important questions for educationalists.

## Critical questions for practice

» If large areas of the brain are devoted to these functions, then in what way do you acknowledge these capacities in your teaching and learning?

» If there are more functioning areas of the brain devoted to the hands than any other part of the body, then why is this capacity not fully utilised for learning?

These are significant questions that will be explored in this chapter.

## The importance of movement

Early adaptative developments by humans have evolved as survival strategies for two significant challenges, notably (1) searching for (moving towards) food and (2) avoiding (moving away) predators. These challenges are more significant than we think: they are responsible for the early development of core human capacities to learn. This is illustrated with reference to animal brains. Basking sharks, for example, have a lower brain capacity than predatory sharks, and, similarly, as a large sedentary mammal foraging on bamboo, the gorilla has a lower brain capacity than the chimpanzee (Allman, 2000). The research mentioned in chapter 1 on the enlarged hippocampus in London taxi drivers, by Maguire et al. (2000), was initiated by the discovery that birds that hide food for the winter have larger brains than birds that didn't hide food. It is also interesting that the *'history of psychology is, in part, a history of how rats learn to find their way in a maze'* (Dudchenko, 2010, p 9). Movement and space are important aspects of learning.

Many areas of the brain are in fact devoted to movement. Gattis argues that the cognitive structures that have been developed over a long period of time to enable us to perceive, navigate, and remember space are now the essential foundations required for abstract cognitive tasks (Gattis, 2001). Many of the illustrative design examples that follow reveal how movement in space is foundational in experiential learning design for education.

Several important changes to the human capacity to learn occurred about 4 million years ago (mya), when early humans moved from a quadrupedal to bipedal lifestyle. The hands were freed from their locomotive function to play a significant part of bodily (embodied) learning, enabling the manipulation of objects, and the execution of complex tasks. Simultaneously the body developed greater spatial awareness along with improvements in specific human sensory capacities. The nervous system, having developed a protective myelin sheath, became capable of much faster processing (thinking) speeds, with reduced signal contamination. These faster processing speeds allowed for greater brain-body coordination and integration, and during the period of crafting tools over 2 mya, spatial coordination and spatial cognition advanced considerably, as did the cerebral cortex, which became capable of higher-level executive functions such as reasoning, planning, decision making, and imagination. Bigger human brains require longer maturity time, and social grouping became important for protection, safety, and collaborative work. Complex social relations developed, giving rise to intricate communication, group coordination, and emotional interactions.

# The contribution of ancient philosophers

By fast-forwarding to more recent centuries to consider how the term 'experience' has been examined, understood, and misunderstood, the comprehension of experiential learning can be improved. Experience and learning are complex words: put them together and the complexity increases. Ancient philosophers, from the East and West, explored these terms, and questioned the role that experience plays in terms of how we make sense of, and learn from, our two worlds (the inner, private embodied world and the embedded world 'out there' that we *in*habit). It has been suggested that experiential learning may have origins in the work of Greek philosophers such as Aristotle, Socrates, and Plato (Stonehouse et al., 2011). Aristotle, the empiricist, argued that we can only know the world through that which is presented to our senses. Socrates focused on learning through questioning and social interaction, whilst Plato, the rationalist, focused on argument and logic. Although these philosophers had differing views, collectively they identified three significant philosophies concerning the way humans learn to make sense of their world: (1) social interaction, (2) sensory-bodily capacities, and (3) the use of logical thinking and argument (cognition). However, it is important to note that these philosophers argued that workers and slaves required only basic training for their jobs; Aristotle *'explicitly excluded women and slaves from higher stages of education'* (Palmer, 2001, p 18), and he also believed that the source of thinking was the heart.

Contrasting philosophical principles emerged from Confucian, Taoist, and Buddhist traditions to create distinct Eastern foundational underpinnings to experiential learning. The aphorism: 'I hear, I forget; I see, I remember; I do, I understand', is derived from Confucian thought originally written in the rich picture-based Chinese language. The English translation fails to embrace the depth of meaning of the original pictographic form. In the USA, Edgar Dale interpreted this translation to create the simple 'Tell, Show, and Do' Instructional Triangle that is familiar to many teachers (Dale, 1969). This translation adds to misguided views that experiential learning is concerned with 'doing' and being 'active'. The Confucian aphorism suggests something richer: immersion, practice, dedication, and discovery, of an attitude, a skill, or knowledge (see Beard and Wilson, 2018). Further critical analysis, later in this and subsequent chapters, will expose other aspects of misunderstanding.

## Developments in the 20th century

Experiential learning is a concept that has had considerable influence beyond education. In the late 19th and early 20th centuries, Western literature identified several key developments that influenced two distinctive threads, notably experiential education, with a focus on schooling, and experiential learning with a focus on adults: both terms frequently overlap and intertwine. On closer examination, five specific areas appear to have developed during this time, broadly positioned within:

> (1) concerns about repressive teaching methods in schools (e.g. Dewey, 1938), with new ideas suggesting that schools adopt, for example, Scientific Methods, Participative approaches, and Heuristics (meaning discovery) (Wight, 1970; Curtis, 1963);
>
> (2) concerns about the ability of young people to survive during times of war gave rise to calls for greater resilience, and strength of character to be

schooled through outdoor, adventure, and nature education (Veevers and Allison, 2011);

(3) the need for nature study and environmental awareness in schools by educator-naturalists (e.g. Rousseau);

(4) adult social action using sensitivity 'training' for human relations, 'laboratory' research with community groups exploring racism, for example (Lewin, 1951);

(5) concerns about managers being overly focused on 'active doing' from research data on management learning styles as part of a popular rise in 'plan, do, review' circular models of the 1960s and 1970s (Taylor, 1991), which were foundational to the emergence of training cycles (Boydell, 1971) and learning cycles (Kolb et al., 1971; Wight, 1970; Torbert, 1972).

Circular models were based, to an extent, on the cyclical scientific processes of: hypothesis, experiment, review and rethink, and reapply. All five of the threads outlined previously expose common objectives for 'liberatory' reform, as foundational to wider educational, social and political change.

Specific narratives have become dominant, with a few individuals perceived as having made a significant contribution to experiential learning and experiential education. In terms of school classroom education, concerns about poor teaching methods were expressed as early as 1900 by the US educator John Dewey, who was critical of the traditional rote, recital, and regurgitation methods, used alongside strict, repressive discipline (see also Wight, 1970). In his 1938 publication, Dewey argued that pupils should be exposed to more constructivist methods, such as the 'scientific method' of 'discovery', as this would lead to a more democratic society. Less well-known is the work of the educational reformist Professor Armstrong, who simultaneously called for the Heuristic Method to be introduced in UK schools (Curtis, 1963). These ideas, of Dewey and less well publicised 'others', were characterised as excessively progressive by traditional, conservative educationalists.

In Physical and Outdoor Education, a 'New Educational Fellowship' emerged out of mounting criticism of educational systems. The well-known educational reformist, Kurt Hahn, arrived in the UK in 1933, following his arrest in Germany, to initiate several enterprises which influenced the field of outdoor 'experiential education' (see Veevers and Allison, 2011). Hahn, concerned about 'social diseases' (Richards, 1999), played a central role in the establishment of post-war initiatives concerned with resilience and character development, including Gordonstoun School (Scotland), the Duke of Edinburgh Award, United World colleges, and Outward Bound (see Parry and Allison, 2021). Interestingly in some parts of the globe, experiential learning is incorrectly perceived as synonymous with outdoor adventure learning.

In the field of management learning, David Kolb and colleagues, building on and synthesising the work of Dewey, Lewin, Piaget, and others, developed what he termed an 'experiential learning theory', in conjunction with the 'experiential learning cycle' (Kolb et al., 1971). Kolb, a cognitive psychologist, and previously professor of organisational behaviour at Sloan School of Management, reworks these earlier influential works to produce an account of learning that is fundamentally cognitivist. Kolb, the most well publicised contributor to experiential learning, initially created what he terms the experiential learning theory with two other academics, though the widespread following of this specific understanding of 'experiential' learning, linked to research on management learning, is often attributed only to Kolb. The focus on management learning by Kolb et al. (1971) occurred at a time when few management qualifications existed, and the research was influenced by systems thinking, problem solving, plan-do-evaluate cycles, feedback loops, and the scientific method (the latter Dewey suggested should be widely used in schools). At this time, *'rational scientific management was spreading rapidly'* (Taylor, 1991, p 259) also influencing the work of Kolb and others. Managers were perceived as being caught in an 'activity trap', with little reflection as to the effectiveness of their actions. Because managers tended to emphasise active experimentation over reflective observations, Kolb and his students later developed management 'learning styles'. Ironically students and staff in universities often refer to the need to gain work experience in 'the real world', 'out there'. This notion is somewhat ironic given this academic research to improve management learning. Such thinking also suggests the university is somehow not real. Such thinking devalues the contribution universities make to the broader lifewide and lifelong learning ecology, that includes not only creating new knowledge, but also developing professionals, including medical training, initiating and conducting research, influencing the economy, and social institutions, including the community, and connecting with and influencing other important global phenomena (see also Barnett, 2018).

Kolb argues (1984) that experience needs to be transformed by reflection to create knowledge – this remains central to his theory of experiential learning. Holman et al. (1997, p 139) are critical of this approach, noting that *'Thinking is seen as separate from experiencing and action; action follows thought and a new dualism is created – reflection and thinking'*. Kolb created a circular model as a popular learning sequence, though initially this consisted of two concentric circles (Kolb and Fry, 1975) to highlight the similarities with the 'problem-solving cycle' developed earlier by Pounds (1965).

# Critical issue

## Understanding contextual settings in the history of experiential learning

During the 1950s and 1960s, the popularity of stimulus-response animal ethology studies diminished, and cognitivism emerged as a dominant paradigm of learning. At this time circular thinking models became commonplace and were adopted by professionals associated with learning. An article in *Management Education and Development* titled 'The Systematic Training Model: Corn Circles in Search of a Spaceship' (Taylor, 1991, p 258) exposes the extent to which these simplistic cyclical models were uncritically adopted:

*They first began to appear about 25 years ago. Neatly laid-out circles in the pages of training textbooks, journals and Industrial Training Board publications. They quickly came to seize the imagination of a growing band of training professionals. They must have been created by a superior intelligence, being so neat and logical and all. There were of course variations in the patterns observed, but these, it was discovered, were due to differing environmental conditions. Being a pragmatic and opportunist bunch the practitioners, although faintly curious about where they came from, what they actually meant, and who controlled them, were so much more interested in associating themselves with the phenomena so as to establish their own professional credibility and status. The mystery and novelty soon became displaced as attempts were made to elaborate and integrate the phenomenon into the known universe. Within a few short years the 'systematic training model' [or 'training cycle' to some] became the orthodoxy of the training profession.*

### Simple and popular

Although the 'learning cycle' was popularised by Kolb, it is identical to that created earlier by Lewin, and difficult to distinguish from other 'experiential' cycles of this period. In 1970, Wight also published an Experiential Learning Model, initially as a ten-stage cycle, but this was later simplified. Wight argued that experiential learning was important to 'participative' pedagogic methods, noting that '*in experiential learning the emphasis is on creative problem-solving, a process involving steps or phases*' (p 23). Wight (1970, p 11) notes the term '*Participative Education was borrowed from the trends in industry toward Participative Management*'.

Prior to the learning cycle developed by Kolb, Boydell, who worked in Sheffield Business School in the UK, developed a pioneering ten-stage 'Systematic Training Cycle', as a circular model (see Boydell, 1971), which was later simplified to four stages. In 1976, Boydell wrote a monograph titled *Experiential Learning*, where he positions 'rote' versus 'discovery' and 'meaningful' versus 'expository' learning as diametrically opposed forces. This is significant as these four terms represent some of the key concerns at play in education at this time in the history of experiential education. Boydell references Borton's model (1970) of a 'Learning Process', which was also simple, pragmatic, and easy to remember. This three-step reflective questioning approach asks: *What?* (did we do?), *So What?* (what does this mean for us?), *Now What?* (what happens next?). This was widely adopted by outdoor facilitators. Also popular with outdoor facilitators is the simple four-stage reviewing cycle: *experience, express, examine,* and *explore* by Greenaway (Greenaway, 1993). Greenaway demonstrated through his extensive research and practice that review and reflection can also be designed as an active, productive process. This way, reflection can become a 'concrete experience': Levitin (2020, p 55) suggests *'the key to remembering things is to get involved in them actively. ... Actively using information, generating and regenerating it, engages more areas of the brain than merely listening'*. Interestingly Cell (1984) considers reflection as not separate but a process of continuous interpretation and reinterpretation in and on experiences.

When 'experiential learning' is entered into search engines, the algorithms imply that one author is responsible for developing a 'theory' of experiential learning. This generates an important critical question as to why specific models, theories, and voices about experiential learning have emerged as dominant narratives. One partial explanation can be found in *Top Brain Bottom Brain* (Kosslyn and Miller, 2013), where a chapter titled 'Sweeping Claims' addresses the question as to why Nobel prize winning research on the left and right hemisphere by Roger Sperry gave rise to numerous uninformed 'popularist ideas', why they persisted for so long, and why a Google search on the topic results in millions of 'hits'. The authors suggest that whilst internet algorithms play an important role:

*The answer may lie in our instinctive search for understanding, a timeless narrative of the human experience. As a species, we seem to be hardwired to try to make*

> sense of what we encounter, even something as complex as the brain – and so we create narratives, simplifying them when necessary. That is not a bad thing, provided that the narratives are simplified in the right way – characterising core ideas and not introducing misconceptions.
>
> (Kosslyn and Miller, 2013, pp 69–70)

# Experiential learning: liberatory intentions and prejudice

Historical evidence from the 19th and early 20th centuries suggests that many early contributors held prejudicial views about the exclusion of slaves, women, and working people from education, i.e. those often without voice, power, or financial resources. The following quotation, taken from *The History of Education in Great Britain*, highlights prejudicial views published in a government pamphlet in 1867:

*The lower classes ought to be educated to discharge the duties cast upon them. They should also be educated that they may appreciate and defer to a higher cultivation when they need it, and the higher classes ought to be educated in a very different manner, in order that they may exhibit to the lower classes a higher education to which, if it was shown to them, they would bow down and defer.*

(Curtis, 1963, p 256)

These comments came from Robert Lowe. Educated at Winchester and Oxford, he became Vice-President at the Department of Education. He was associated with the introduction of educational efficiencies and 'Payment by Results' (performance measures related to income received).

# Silenced voices: *his*-tory and *her*-story

By his own admission, Dewey lamented later in his life that he had achieved little change in the schools of America (Lillard, 2017). It is not known whether Dewey was influenced by the Italian educationalist Montessori, who is referred to by Swinderski (2011) as the Mother of Experiential Education. Montessori set up an 'unofficial' school in 1907, in a house that was supported by funds to enable her to teach 'ordinary' children. Montessori was so successful with these institutionalised children referred to as 'idiots' that she was able to get many of them to pass the 'normal' exams that the 'ordinary' children took. Despite qualifying as a doctor when women were not allowed to pursue such a career, her success in education encountered considerable resistance from conservative, establishment males. Although her work remains less well-known than Dewey, her experiential pedagogy continues to be influential in primary classrooms (Lillard, 2017), and in 2023 a film, *La Nouvelle Femme*, made its debut on the big screen to honour her remarkable achievements.

A critical examination of the influence of Kurt Hahn on outdoor and adventure education exposes the work of another lesser-known female who contributed to the evolution of experiential education. Gray and Mitten (2018) highlight recent research that uncovers the significant contribution made by Marina Ewald: now each year a significant outdoor experiential educator is nominated to speak in celebration of the achievements of Marina Ewald. In 2022, an adaptation of the Holistic Experiential Learning Theory (HELT; Beard, 2023) was central to the Ewald speech by nominee Vishwas Parchure of The Experiential Institute, India.

Gray and Mitten (2018) suggest that the *his*tory of outdoor learning has been 'genderwashed' by male domination.

# Experiential learning in the 21st century

Whilst circular models reached a peak in the 1970s, their popularity waned by the early 1990s (Boydell, 1976; Seaman, 2008; Taylor, 1991). By the late 20th and early 21st centuries, new thinking about experiential learning began to surface within a wide range of disciplines, with new thinking recommending a more discerning, whole-person pedagogic trajectory with a broader ontological rather than epistemological understanding of learning. This is the case with the collective critiques of the work of Kolb: they too call for a broader, holistic trajectory for experiential learning in the 21st century. Some of these critical commentaries are briefly outlined next.

## Critical question for practice

Why has the work of the medical profession, and the substantial research on the brain and the body, and their role in learning, not been recognised in the history of experiential learning?

# Academic critiques and calls for change

One of the central concerns of this book is to improve the understanding of what is meant by a learning 'experience'. Critical commentaries offer new foundations on which to build future theories of experiential learning.

Dewey called for the creation of a 'theory of experience', and according to Crosby (1995, p 11), Dewey maintained that *'we find ourselves in continual transaction with the physical, psychological, mental, spiritual world, and philosophy should be a systematic investigation into the nature of this experience'*. This is a particularly significant quotation that points out that Dewey also suggested a multi-disciplinary perspective for understanding the experience of learning.

Elana Michelson and Tara Fenwick have both produced innovative critical thinking about experiential learning. Michelson (1998), a critical feminist, questions the way Kolb privileges mind over body and the lack of recognition of the role of the body as a site of knowledge. Fenwick (2003) is critical of the suggestion by Kolb that 'knowledge' is somehow extracted and abstracted from experience. Fenwick, like Dewey, suggests that experiential learning should be understood as involving the whole person *'physically, emotionally, sensually, mentally and perhaps spiritually'* (p 13), as a permanent state of construction rather than something concrete and knowable. Fenwick explores four theoretical orientations for experiential learning in addition to the experience-reflect-learn constructivist theory from Kolb. They are 'situative theories' (place and participating communities of practice), 'psychoanalytic theories' (for example unconscious desires and ego), and 'complexity theories' (exploring the complexities of systems thinking/ecological relationships).

In *Beyond Learning by Doing: Theoretical Currents in Experiential Education*, Roberts (2012, p 14) argues that *'constructivist models reduce the highly interactive and bodily qualities of outdoor and adventure experiences to secondary elements in an individual's experience'*. Others argue that the learning cycle is overly mechanistic and formulaic, with undue focus on cognition in a way that downplays the importance of other modes of learning (Moon, 2004; Seaman, 2008; Holman et al., 1997; Fenwick, 2003; Michelson, 1998; Roberts, 2012). Miettinen suggests that the work of Kolb fits well into business school consulting literature, and that his work can also be interpreted as a form of *'marketing promotion'* (2000, p 5).

Learning is not confined to a few core capacities such as the thinking brain. Davis and Sumara (1997) suggest that any enquiry into the 'experience' of learning should not focus *'on the components of experience but, rather, on the relations that bind these elements together in action'* (p 108). Feelings, sensing, and thinking; the body-mind partnership; human culture and politics; and individual and/or group interactions are just a few of the interacting factors that continually influence the 'experience' of learning. In this vein, and in a similar way to Fenwick, Davis and Sumara suggest that cognition does not reside solely in the mind of the individual, and they question what might happen if learning is considered in ways other than from a constructivist orientation:

[What would happen] *if we were to reject the self-evident axiom that cognition is located within cognitive agents who are cast as isolated from one another and distinct from the world, and insist instead that all cognition exists in the interstices of a complex ecology of organismic relationality?*

(Davis and Sumara, 1997, p 110)

Fenwick positions this work by Davis and Sumara within the theoretical orientation of complexity theories, as an orientation that recognises that humans continually act and interact within a fluid, overlapping, interconnected experiential ecology. These interactions comprise the psychological, biological, personal, social, and cultural: Fenwick notes that this orientation focuses on a 'co-emergence' of all the systems. From this perspective, thinking does not occur separately from belonging, being, or acting in the world: human experience operates within large social networks where norms and values are negotiated within relationships, and within complex societal, historical, and environmental frames involving agency, power, and politics. Contemporary theories and modelling of 'experiential' learning should ideally reflect these calls for greater complexity. Holman et al. (1997, p 145) conclude that *'as long as the predominant learning theory is seen in terms of Kolb's experiential learning theory, management learning and educational practices will always be caught in the problems associated with cognitivism'*.

# A new holistic experiential learning model for the 21st century

It becomes apparent that a 'whole'-person pedagogy is widely called for, as necessary for experiential learning to advance in the 21st century. It is for this reason that a new Holistic Experiential Learning Theory (HELT) is introduced here, together with new design modelling underpinned by my extensive practice, and with a comprehensive theoretical justification for this model presented in *Experiential Learning Design: Theoretical Foundations and Effective Principles* (Beard, 2023). This modelling, as a contemporary theory of experiential learning, recognises seven overlapping experiencing capacities: belonging in both the social and more than human world, doing, sensing, feeling, knowing, and being in the world. 'Be-longing' and 'be-ing' clearly have a linguistic connection. Each of these seven capacities for learning are complex. Sensing, for example, incorporates many sub-level modes of visual, haptic, auditory, kinaesthetic, olfactory, spatial awareness, and many other sensory modes. 'Doing' is a general linguistic term coined to embrace behaviour, agency, production, building and constructing, and co-production, etc. The following modelling is a simple representation, as a re-presentation of reality: it is difficult to create a visual format that highlights the continual oscillation and integration of these core aspects of experiencing the world. Belonging and being, presented at the two ends of the model, need to be understood as connected: there is an element of complex integration in the potential circularity.

Experiential learning is progressively envisaged as involving a broader holistic base of human experiential capacities, beyond unsophisticated cognitive notions that involve a reflective, structured cycle, whereby knowledge is processed and extracted after the experience. Experiential learning variably engages immediate, immersive, embodied, enacted, embedded, and participatory encounters. Seen in this way, it becomes evident that learning unfolds dynamically. The notion of a 'learning experience ecology' may be helpful for educational practice.

The senses are pivotal in connecting the outer world experience with the inner world experience. The senses are particularly important to awareness raising processes that support positive mental health and well-being, as discussed in chapter 6.

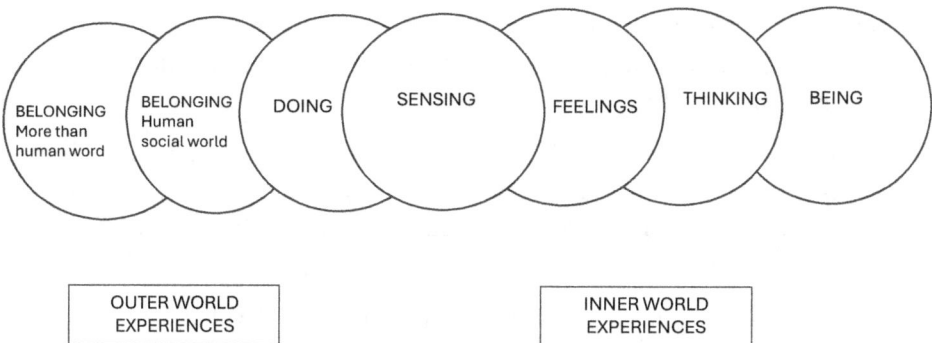

**Figure 2.1** The Holistic Experiential Learning Theory: seven capacities for learning

> **Example 2.1**
>
> ### Understanding complexity and the state of flux
>
> With reference to the seven modes of experiencing shown in Figure 2.1, let me highlight the reality of an integrated, holistic understanding of 'experience' by asking you to imagine holding the top rim of a glass or mug with your hand. What do you experience? The experience is not a separate sensation of each finger and a thumb; rather, all of these sensations are integrated to form a whole, i.e. the feeling of the glass as being circular.
>
> Now try a second experience. Touch the fingertips of your right hand with the fingertips of your left hand. Now separate them and do it once more. You will notice that you cannot feel the fingertips of one hand without the fingertips of the other. This helps to understand reciprocity. There is no 'outer world' without the 'inner world' and vice versa, and all of these seven experiencing capacities cannot occur in isolation.

Finally, on a thought-provoking note, the first 'People's College' was opened in Sheffield in 1842, and later, '*in order to place it on a firm basis, they recognized it under a committee and drew up a new set of regulations which put the government of the college into the hands of the students*' (Curtis, 1967, p 478). Even in the 21st century this would be seen as a very radical decision to empower students.

> # Summary
>
> - This chapter highlights how experiential learning design has been shaped by a long and troubled history involving power, politics, and promotion. The story so far has been limited to the contributions of a few individuals.
>
> - Historically concerned with liberation and emancipation, experiential learning is often perceived as 'progressive' and 'radical'. Experiential learning has faced opposition from conservative educationalists who seek to preserve traditional ways.
>
> - A brief review of some of the main contributors to the development of experiential learning highlights how a few *his*-tories have dominated and overshadowed *her*-stories.

- The chapter argues that current theorising and modelling of experiential learning design is overly simplistic, and so a more complex, Holistic Experiential Learning Theory and modelling is presented.

## Useful texts

Lillard, A (2017) (3rd edition) *Montessori: The Science Behind the Genius.* New York: Oxford University Press.

*This book explores in detail the underpinning research that shows how and why the experiential approaches adopted by Montessori in the teaching of children were so successful.*

Fenwick, T J (2003) *Learning Through Experience: Troubling Orthodoxies and Intersecting Questions.* Malabar, Florida: Krieger Publishing Company.

*This book explores several different perspectives on* experiential *learning and asks some difficult questions about what experiential learning really is.*

# Chapter 3 | Designs that utilise the core student capacities for learning

## Introduction

This chapter introduces some basic practical steps to start the design processes for student learning experiences. New design principles and design structures are introduced, including the learning route maps and design zones, and the link between learning objectives and choreography. The chapter also focuses on navigation, tracking, and scaffolding designs that support student learning in Higher Education.

## Starting to design: when, where, and how?

As teachers we are all designers of learning experiences, balancing the technical-rational objectives and outcomes with the choreographic processes that bring the objectives to life. Time for experience design is underestimated or neglected in work-loading systems, yet the investment is rewarded in the long term through student achievements, positive reviews, and reduced delivery pressure. Working at a leading University in Malaysia I asked academic staff to comment on the significant things they noticed after three days of working with them on learning design. The unanimous comment from the group was: *'you didn't seem to do much!'*. Music to my ears: this was what I had intended as the hard work is in the design. Their comments included their enjoyment of the experience, how fast the three days had gone, how much they had learned, and how much they appreciated the need to 'teach' less because they were shown how to *'let the students experience (do) the learning'*.

### Critical questions for practice

» How much time do you spend on designing your student learning experience?

» In the design of your 'teaching', to what extent do you focus on letting your students do (experience) the learning?

» Do you feel you could improve your design knowledge and design skills?

## Liberating structures

Module guides present the details of lectures and seminars, with times, dates, and topics, in 'grid-style' formats: these documents are mainly for planning and administrative purposes rather than supporting students. They are 'representations' (see Verschaffel et al., 2010), and they typically flow from top to bottom: in a functional sense this approach poorly represents the student learning journey. By utilising research on the way humans think about space (spatial cognition), maps can better represent modules or programmes to students in more useful, liberating ways. Maps existed as a means of communication long before speech and text (Gattis, 2001). Carefully designed maps can improve navigational functionality and enhance student engagement. In *Transition into Higher Education*, Jones et al. (2023) frequently refer to student transition as a process of students navigating change as they move within and through formal education, and navigation is used in the title of a book on student transition by Gale and Parker (2014). Navigation, learning journey, moving forwards, and other linguistic (spatial) metaphors present design clues for improving your student learning experience. Developing a heightened linguistic awareness is important in learning design.

To get started, bear in mind there is always a beginning, a middle, and an end. Finkel reinforces this notion, noting: *'if we aim to design a sustained learning experience for students, we will do well to give the experience some shape through time. We need to provide a beginning, a middle, and an end'* (2000, p 94). To do this, use a long sheet of paper (e.g. lining wallpaper) to construct the design, preferably doing it as a collaborative endeavour with other staff members, and, if possible, with students. Sketch out a simple three-zone structure: each zone will contain very different experiences.

## Starting at the end

Start to the right of the *end* zone, where (*anticipated*) learning objectives-outcomes are first written. The objectives usually start with: 'By the *end* of X,Y,Z ... students will be able to ...'. They are the 'promise' we make to students. Working backwards these objectives are *deconstructed*, broken down into the component parts, like a jigsaw. The component parts are the more detailed experience design that will lead to students *arriving* (*journey* metaphor) at the objectives. However, a choreography of the experience is required, and it is a big leap from writing objectives to the design of a good student learning experience.

In experiential designs, objectives are met through an 'acquaintance with' as opposed to just 'knowledge of' the subject, so design to: 'Let the Learners do (= experience) the

| A. **Three Zones** | | |
|---|---|---|
| Beginning | Middle | Ending |

A five-zone design could be used to include a before, beginning, middle, end, and after as shown next.

| B. **Five Zones** | | | | |
|---|---|---|---|---|
| Pre | Beginning | Middle | Ending | Post |

The map is then populated with appropriate information to support students without extraneous cognitive load.

| C. **Developing the Learning Route Map** | | |
|---|---|---|
| Beginning | Middle | Ending |

The bottom line of the previous box becomes the line on which to overlay the experience map.

Design creates a flow of experiences from left to right with details of each specific experience.

**Figure 3.1** Three basic design structures

Learning'. The sequence, direction, and flow of learning experiences is important, for example the shape and flow of a meeting is like a diamond, in that meetings open up and then close down.

Design simultaneously addresses two aspects: experiences *for* learning, and the experience *of* learning. Let me explain. Experience design '*for*' learning allows the student to learn *from* having a specific experience such as making or producing something. Taking the important concept of students '*producing*' something, such as a podcast, or an audio recording of their critical conversation about a topic, a database, etc. This experience of producing something does not in itself ensure that good learning occurs: tutors must also have a good understanding of how humans learn and this should be intertwined with the learning arising out of producing something. It is the design '*of*' learning, both as the experience unfolds and afterwards. These processes should ideally utilise several student capacities (thinking, sensing, feelings, belonging, doing, etc.). A simple example might be to apply cognitive scaffolding that supports thinking and enables students to 'grasp' something. This could be as simple as requiring students to place a coloured disc on something to create a category, or place a set of arrows between objects in a way that promotes discussion about relational and conceptual understanding of two concrete objects (see chapters 4 and 5). In mathematics, manipulatives are used as navigational scaffolding tools to make thinking, sensing, or feelings visible. Making learning visible is a good design approach, in that it enables staff to hear, see, and understand what and whether the students are learning. This principle can become the foundational basis of experiential assessment.

# Designing zone experiences

Typically, the first (beginning) design zone includes getting started, student belonging, attachment, relational learning, and affiliation. In this design zone, particularly with new students, it is important to develop strong peer and tutor relationships that support identity creation (see Bingham and Sidorkin, 2004). This zone is also about introductions, of staff, students, topics, and the overall shape and flow of the learning journey. These social interactions create a sense of belonging, related to theories of affiliation and attachment (see Baumeister and Leary, 1995; Cassidy, 2016). Exploring power relations, voice, and agency are particularly important at this stage. Strong social bonds, long-term relations, resilience, and transformation are initiated at this early stage (see chapter 6). Remember that many students are also keen to get started on their subject study: it is important not to design introductions that result in students commenting '*that that was a waste of time*'!

## Example 3.1

### Do you introduce yourself to students?

Let the learners do the learning by letting them ask you questions about what they want to know about you? Each small group can ask two questions. Offer advice: ask boring questions and you will get boring answers! Ask interesting questions and you will get interesting answers! This approach to introductions promotes the following: student interaction, learning to ask questions and speaking in front of the whole class, learning about the tutor (professional and personal), promoting relational learning, gaining a sense of voice, agency, and power. I follow this by asking students to do a '15 seconds of fame' video: their first taste of speaking in front of the class. They each have 15 seconds to say their name and say something about themselves or why they chose the topic or field they are studying, for example. This is a really good way for me to get to know student names and to learn something about each student.

The middle design zone advances the topic, moving from simplicity towards complexity: by the end most, if not all, the anticipated learning objectives tend to be achieved. This middle zone has enhanced social interaction and the cognitive ~ affective balance has to be facilitated (~ means complimentary rather than oppositional pairs). The experiences might include producing things (chapter 5): Levitin (2020) suggests that students should be actively generating and regenerating (e.g. co-producing) information they have gained, to engage more areas of the brain. The end zone, in contrast, is often focused on experiences of reflection, review, evaluation, memory enhancement and retention, and celebration.

| BEGINNING | MIDDLE | END |
|---|---|---|
| Starting, student and staff introductions, icebreakers, settling in, belonging regarding people and space (digital/physical classroom), etc., getting to know, anticipation and motivation. Consider social affiliation/attachment/belonging. Consider student anxiety, fear, threat, social exclusion, and safety. Explore power, control, voice, agency, responsibility, security, and a safe, trusting, and positive emotional climate. | Experiences *for* and *of* learning. Design a sequence of experiences that construct learning objectives: building on existing experiences, consider defining parameters, key theories, models, co/creating representations, practical illustrations, simplicity to complexity, experiential wave, skills development, knowledge acquisition, behaviours, critical/conceptual/creative work. Awareness work. Hands-on experiences, acquaintance with. Utilising many core student learning capacities. | Final constructions. Revisiting intended learning objectives, reviewing, reflecting, production, and co-production of review materials, summaries, final questions and answers, memory enhancement (refer to the practical example in chapter 4), ending, networking, evaluating, links to what next, celebrating, and closure. Links to assessment. |

**Figure 3.2** Design zone: illustrative contents

# Navigating the experience

The next stage of design is to create a route map specifically for the students. Utilising journey metaphors, these route maps prevent students getting lost by highlighting their destinations, seeing approaching topics, enabling students to look back at what they have done, and seeing looming assessments! The route map in figure 3.3 was created for a staff development event design for the Education University of Hong Kong. This map communicates their learning journey using combinations of depictive (visually) and descriptive (text) formats, with additional multi-media formats such as colours, shapes, arrows, and a '*you are here*' location pointer. The line below the three zones can become the out-*line* of the route map. The London Underground Map, upon which many global transport maps are based, is said to be one of the most iconic navigational tools ever created, and the designer, Harry Beck, got the idea from looking at the simple electrical wiring in a plug (Schwetman, 2014)! Beck simplified reality, and his route maps offer visually stimulating colours, symbols, lines, emphasis, novelty, icons, images, and keywords as navigational clues. This cartographic representation reduces 'extraneous load' (reduced brain processing).

# Choreography and graphic design

As architects of learning experiences, it is important to be aware of multi-media and cartographic principles (see Mayer, 2014): they can reduce 'Death By Powerpoint'. Multi-'media' design principles can be used to improve route map functionality as

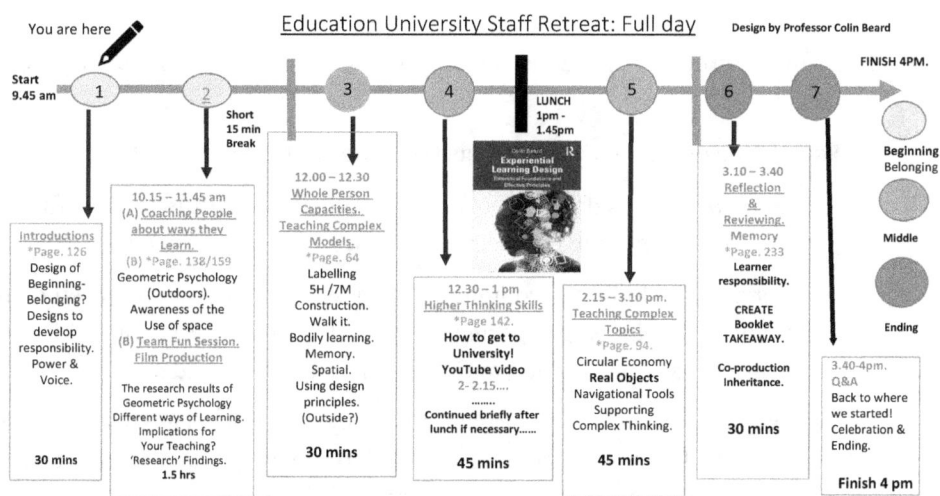

**Figure 3.3** An illustrative route map design

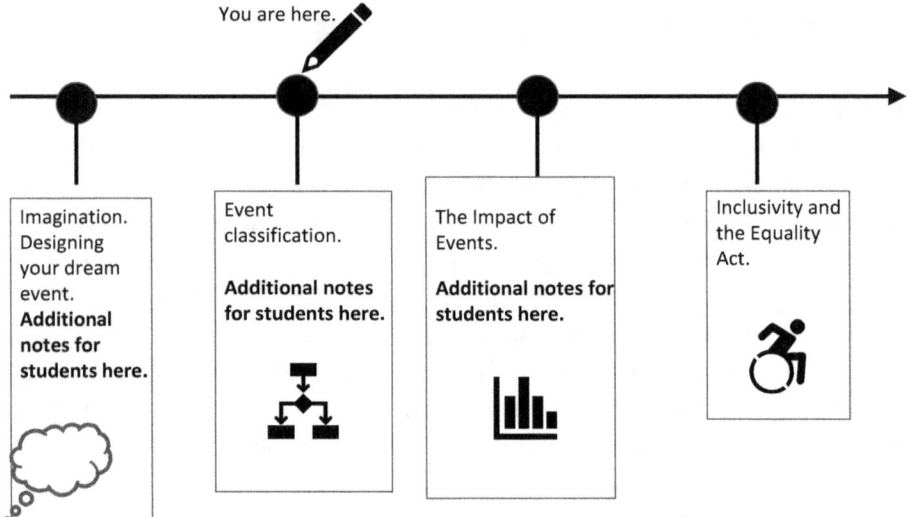

**Figure 3.4** Student engagement and the design of seminar route maps with descriptive text and depictive icons to enhance visual memory triggers

specific navigational formats can be utilised to scaffold student understanding by using navigational interactions.

All learning designs have layers within layers: there are micro and macro experiences, with beginnings, middles, and endings. A specific seminar experience occurs within a broader module experience, within a broader curriculum experience, within the design of a degree. The following eight steps summarise how to start a student learning experience design:

1. Draw a three- or five-zone 'map' (similar to the London Underground design).

2. Start at the end zone with the objectives and return to the start.

3. Break the objectives down (deconstruct) into the constituent parts (like a jigsaw). The parts guide the form of student learning experiences.

4. In the start zone build the content by considering the design of the student beginning and belonging experiences: consider your relationship with students, as well as power, voice, and responsibility are played out.

5. Complete the middle zone (main zone) by designing constituent topic experiences. Reduce the amount of standard delivery-transmission teaching. Utilise designs where the students do the learning (experiencing).

Choreography involves moving from simple to complex designs, as well as the overall design sequence, shape, and flow. Ask yourself: How does this design fit together as a 'whole'?

6. End zone designs concentrate on the part ~ whole relationship (~ means complimentary rather than oppositional pairs). The stage that puts the whole experience together. This phase often includes the final production of something.

7. End zone designs also focus on reflection, review, evaluation, and memory enhancement.

8. Return to the start of the design and re-check the sequence and flow of all the learning experiences.

# Inclusive learning design: harnessing multiple student capacities to learn

Students possess a diverse range of capacities for learning, and it makes sense to harness these. Holistic learning models have traditionally argued that the head (cognition), heart (affective/feelings/emotions), and hands (psychomotor/body/sensing) are three of the most significant capacities for learning. Danish educator Knud Illeris in his book *The Three Dimensions of Learning: Contemporary Learning Theory in the Tension Field Between the Cognitive, the Emotional, and the Social* (2002) argues that cognitive, affective, and social capacities are primarily involved in learning. Child psychiatrist Daniel Siegel adopts a perspective that includes the brain, relationships, and self: this is reflected in the sub-title of one of his books *How Relationships and the Brain Interact to Shape Who We Are* (2015). A detailed examination of the substantial, multi-disciplinary body of literature on human learning suggests that there are many important human capacities utilised in learning. Emerging as most noteworthy are the student abilities to think, to sense, to feel, to act and do, to interact and belong, become, and be. All these capacities overlap, interact, and bind together, through interactions between the student internal and external world experiences.

A different representation created to illustrate these capacities that is not so popular with sociologists, takes the form of the combination lock, with all seven capacities portrayed as cogs (Beard and Wilson, 2005). This was designed to show the infinite number of interactional possibilities: the representation was not intended to present design as a mechanical, deterministic process.

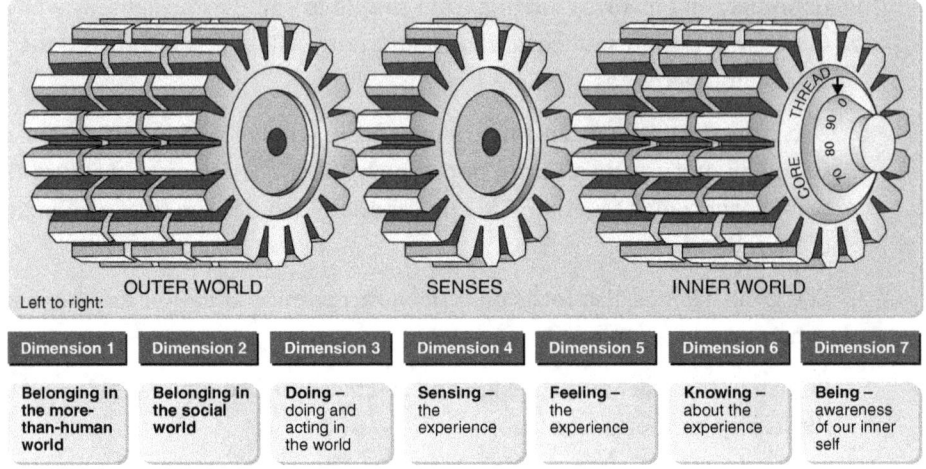

**Figure 3.5** The learning combination lock

# Critical issues

## Embracing the complexity of learning experience design in the 21st century

Peter Jarvis, in his book *Towards a Comprehensive Theory of Human Learning* (2006, p 12), made a candid admission:

*while I am confident that learning is a combination of processes, I now realise that I did not: manage to capture its complexity; depict the person in the world, rather their relationship with the world; relate reason and the emotions….*

This leads to a critical question in relation to teaching and design: do we as teachers rely on overly simplistic models that fail to accommodate the contemporary, complex understanding of how humans learn? Experiential learning is not simply about learning by 'doing', or 'active' learning. It no longer makes sense to consider knowledge as something to be transferred and worked with solely in the mind, as the whole person is actively engaged in learning activities that utilise all the human characteristics. Seven foundational capacities outline the ecological complexity of experiential learning: these capacities are continuously interacting within a flux of change, and with permeable, shifting boundaries. Dashew and Gayeski

(2023, p 257) caution that *'Design is not, strictly, an artistic endeavour. At the same time design is not strictly a science, because artistry and ingenuity are required to engage in design'*. The power of combining the art and science of learning design should not be underestimated.

# A brief introduction to the foundational student capacities for learning

If we fail to acknowledge the true complexity of human learning, then our designs will not be inclusive: one outcome is that some students fail to achieve their full potential. What follows is a very brief introduction to these core capacities for learning.

## The capacities of the student sensing moving body

The human skin, which operates at the interface of the two worlds that we experience, weighs about 15 pounds, and is one of our largest organs. Spread out it is about the size of a double duvet. Significantly, the skin houses major sensory exteroceptors, through which all inbound information passes. The skin acts as the interface between the outside embedded world and inside embodied world of every student. The exteroceptors initiate student engagement through listening, seeing, hearing, touching, smelling, handling, manipulating objects, and other spatial sensory processes. Some senses are expertly utilised for learning in Higher Education, whilst others are neglected. Student attentional focus diminishes rapidly when a specific sensory modality is employed for too long, indeed students refer to 'Death by PowerPoint' as an extreme form of sensory habituation. The student brain is regarded as an *'anticipation machine'*, hungry for contrasting sensory stimulation (Siegel, 2012, p 53), though the senses *'respond only to change or contrast'* (Rowe, 2001, p 50). Significantly, movement triggers attentional focus.

Student listening and reading capacities are important for learning, yet they are prone to the problematic 'Errors of Imagination'. The linguistic challenge to fully describe experiences is in itself problematic, as language is not experience (Sheets-Johnstone, 2011). Speech and text symbolically present information in a linear form that can limit the transmission of complex ideas. Furthermore, when a student reads or listens, a process of imagining occurs: this is nicely illustrated by a poster in the Harry Potter studios in London which says: 'What starts off as WORDS on paper becomes the IMAGES that we conjure up' (caps in the original). People often say that a film they watched turned out to be nothing like the book they read. This imagination gap occurs when we teach by speaking or writing: students imagine what it is we teachers are trying to get across. The cognitive processing of imagination is complex. Zhang and Gee note that:

*it is much as if we can record and experience what we are having, record it as a sort of mental "video" (but one that captures all senses, not just vision) and then store this video in our head. Then we can replay all the videos we have recorded as a form of memory or slice and edit them to create new videos that work as imagination or scenario planning. This is, at base, just what learning is. Learning is the effects of our former experiences – as they are activated and edited – on our futures.*

(Zhang and Gee, 2023, p 2)

Dorothy Rowe illustrates how errors of imagination are further exacerbated when students perceive the world in the way they conceive it:

*The meanings we chose to create arise from all the meanings we have created in the past. The old saying, "if I hadn't seen it I wouldn't have believed it", might be correct in particular circumstances ... but in general the saying should be "if I hadn't believed it I wouldn't have seen it".*

(Rowe, 2001, p 50)

Errors of imagination can be significantly reduced by paying attention to the way learning is enriched by spatial, bodily, and conceptual metaphors (Lakoff and Johnson, 1999). These metaphors create clues for cognitive navigation that scaffold student conceptual understanding. Higher Education, further education, lower marks, feeling down, being close, categories that contain, are examples. Let me explore a very simple visual scaffold in Example 3.2.

## Example 3.2

### Metaphors that scaffold cognition: developing complex thinking

The shapes shown in figure 3.6 are a visual representation used to explain to first-year students how to develop more complex levels of thinking. These depictions (visuals) support teacher descriptions (spoken word) to guide student thinking. Based on the phrase 'multiple points of view', the 'points' in the shapes represent different 'points' of view, representing different perspectives, themes, and arguments, as well as increased complexity. Applying the topic of racism and starting with a straight line, this image represents two simplistic and opposite points of view, i.e. that a student 'views' racism as an issue of colour only (black and white dualism). This would be an unsatisfactory, overly simplistic analysis: racism is a complex phenomenon. Moving clockwise the triangle visually presents three points of view (e.g. colour, class, and culture), demonstrating a slight increase in depth and breadth of understanding. The hexagon image shows six perspectives or points of view: fear, threat, colour, power, culture, and class. This complexity would gain more marks and show a wider understanding of the complexity of racism. The last image represents the messy complexity of racism in real life, inherent within societies today. On closer inspection, this messy complexity has nodal clusters of interest to be explored: these can reveal significant interrelated issues (intersectionality). Students who are introduced to this visual representation will often say they now 'see' what we mean by 'higher', more complex levels of conceptual thinking.

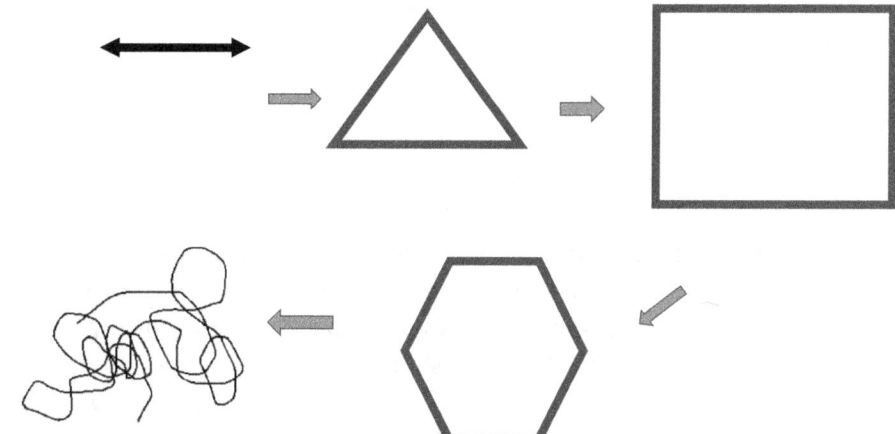

**Figure 3.6** Moving to increased complexity: a visual representation

The student spatial cognitive capacities are often neglected in design. Sheets-Johnstone notes that it is not surprising that *'kinaesthesia is omitted or slighted and that we believe ourselves to have only five senses'* (2009, p 168). Sheets-Johnstone explores detailed evidence that movement and spatial awareness represent the evolutionary roots of human thinking (1990). Research by Maguire et al. (2000) with London taxi drivers was mentioned in an earlier chapter as research offering an insight into human spatial awareness. Their work demonstrates brain plasticity by exposing how a specific area of the brain, linked to spatial memory, expands in experienced taxi drivers. They also found that this area shrank when they retired! Maguire went on to study world memory champions who have long used the ancient 'Method of Loci' or memory journey to remember large amounts of information. Memory champions use this method of memory enhancement by depositing information in specific places, along a known route.

The sense of touch (haptics) is also important for learning: whilst touch is spread over the entire body, the hands are adept at manipulating objects (see Chatterjee and Hannan, 2016 on Object Based Learning – OBL). The hands are adept communicators (see Goldin-Meadow, 2003) and we speak of hands-on experiences. Manipulation by hands creates bodily movement which in turn generates interest, arousal, and attentional focus as the brain and body work together in a superb age-old partnership. The sub-title of a key text on the role of the hands in learning is what the manual tells the mental, highlighting the mistaken dualism that the body does, whilst the brain thinks (Radman, 2013).

Understanding the role of the body in sensing, doing, and thinking is central to the notion of embodied learning. The phrase 'learning by doing' is too simplistic, as is 'active learning'. A richer conception beyond the interpretation of physical 'activity' is required (see Roberts, 2012).

## Student thinking capacities (cognition)

Thought results from '*the activity of billions of cells in the most complex structure in the known universe – the human brain*' (Cobb, 2021, p 15). Yet the basic cells of the brain and spinal cord originate from the outer layers of the embryo that eventually becomes the skin. This explains why Siegel (2007, p 29) comments that the '*brain originates at the interface of the inner and outer worlds of our bodily defined selves*'. Neuroscientist Levitin (2020, p 282) notes that '*the body influences the mind just as the mind influences the body. Embodied cognition puts intelligence and control out in the body*'.

As mentioned in chapter 2, Lakoff and Nunez (2000, p 1), in their book, *Where Mathematics Comes From: How the Embodied Mind Brings Mathematics Into Being*, note that '*most of the brain is devoted to vision, motion, spatial understanding, interpersonal interaction, coordination, emotions, language, and everyday reasoning*'. This quotation highlights several capacities that need to be utilised in holistic approaches to 'experiential' learning design. Perceptual and motor systems play an important role in thinking (cognition). The more we fire specific sets of neurons the more we remember. Levitin (2020, p 55) suggests that:

*the key to remembering things is to get involved in them actively. Passively learning something, such as listening in a lecture, is a sure way to forget it. Actively using information, generating, and regenerating it, engages more areas of the brain then merely listening.*

## Example 3.3

### Active experiential memory enhancement

Students can actively experience memory enhancement, for example, by using their Learning Route Map to generate (co-produce) their own module memory handbook. At the end of a module, for example, students can create a seminar audio recording by passing a recording device along a physical line (masking tape) with numbered stations on it to represent each route map seminar session. A group of three or four students stand at a chosen station and record what was experienced and what they learned in that seminar. This is then posted to the group as a group digital audio format, and it can be translated into a written document using speech recognition. The students take responsibility for producing memory enhancing audios or booklets.

Neuro*diversity* is a term that acknowledges that students are all 'wired' in completely different ways and we think in different ways. Humans possess billions of different neuronal processing patterns (nerves), and each of the billions of neurons link to around a thousand other neurons in the brain. The nervous system spreads into the equally diverse body. The senses are diverse as are interactions with the social world. All the capacities shape who we are, and what we pay attention to (see McGilchrist, 2009).

The complex brain has a top and bottom, a front and back, and a left and right side: integration and separation of processing functions occur in all these areas. The notion of attentional focus is particularly important in that the brain is split into two parts and there must be a reason for this. In evolutionary processes, vertebrates developed eyes either side of the head, and ornithological research in particular highlights how birds had to focus on the details of feeding whilst at the same time paying attention to the predators in the sky. This meant that attentional focus had to be divided. Areas of the left brain (in an evolutionary sense) evolved to pay more attention to detail, whilst the right hemisphere developed an ability to better attend to the bigger picture.

# Student emotions and feelings (affective capacities)

Emotions are relational experiences that have evolved to play a significant role in arousal, attentional focus, and motivation (including motivation to learn). Levitin (2020, p 147) notes that:

*Like perception, emotions appear to be constructed out of bits and pieces of experience and inference, and the job of our brains is to tie the disparate threads together and try and make sense of what's happening around us and inside us.*

Emotions are reactions of the mind (cognitive) played out in the theatre of the body: emotion contains the word motion, and we say 'we are moved by something ...'. Attending to affective experiences is an important skill for teachers (Beard et al., 2007): the emotional climate is shaped by important elements such as the behaviour of the teachers and students, materials, and activities. Human mirror neurons enable significant social interactions in that we can feel and sense the emotions of others, to develop empathy. Mortiboys (2002), in *The Emotionally Intelligent Lecturer*, suggests that design for positive emotional climate for learning is important, and he recommends openly asking questions about feelings associated with a favourite learning experience. Ideal answers he suggests might include enthusiastic, fascination, happy and alive, being valued, confident, curious, and excited. Evolutionary psychology offers insights into the negative threat brain emotions of stress, fear, and anxiety (Gilbert, 2010), that can create mental health issues. Negative experiences of learning, rather than positive ones, are more often the subject of research. There are also more negative words in most languages (Baumeister et al., 2001). Positive emotions serve to counterbalance negative emotions, and they broadly separate into achievement (incentive, resource-seeking, drive-excitement system), as a pleasurable 'high' (dopamine), whereas social interaction and friendships (e.g. affiliation/security/belonging) result in a positive 'calming' (natural opiates/endorphins). The pleasurable emotions of student learning are rarely discussed, though research suggests that creating more student awareness of their passion, commitment, and pleasure is important (see Beard et al., 2014).

Pink advocates that happiness results from being productive, having pleasurable experiences that create purpose (2010): these three Ps offer opportunities for reframing learning in Higher Education. A balanced emotional self can result in greater resilience, reduced mental health issues, and positive well-being (Siegel, 2007). Emotional responses to learning are important aspects of the student experience of belonging.

> ## Critical question for practice
>
> To what extent do you intentionally design for a specific emotional climate for your students?

## Social interactions and social belonging

Holmes and Slade (2018) note that affective exchange underpins the fabric of social life, and Jones et al. (2023, p 6), referring to transition in Higher Education, note: *'If students are to successfully navigate their first year, universities need to recognise the cognitive processes of belonging, where students negotiate emotion and a sense of attachment to the community and institution.'*

Theories of attachment and affiliation are particularly significant to understanding social interaction (Bowlby, 1969; Cassidy, 2016): social interaction plays a significant role in both transition and transformation. Relational learning, a growing area of pedagogic research, focuses on the involvement of peers and teachers in the collaborative co-creation of learning (Bovill, 2020). Students are social beings, possessing a deep need to belong (Baumeister and Leary, 1995). The sense of belonging (*be*-longing) also relates to the spaces and places where learning takes place, whether digital or physical, or both, in classrooms, on campus, and beyond. In physical spaces, teachers have traditionally controlled 'front' spaces where power is held: students sit at the back. Classrooms with multi-directional designs can facilitate shifts in power, and resource use. This sense of belonging is foundational to student learning, as is friendship; both provide a sense of psychological security.

Nearly three decades ago in an Italian neuroscience laboratory, mirror neurons were discovered by chance when first, as expected, every time a monkey grasped a peanut the expected neurons fired, and the very same visuomotor neurons fired when the monkeys watched someone else move peanuts towards their mouth, even if the monkey had not moved at all. Mirror neurons have since been linked with socio-emotional aspects of learning and cognitive empathy, explaining the ability to *'imagine and understand another person's thoughts, intentions, and feelings'* (Butera and Aziz-Zadeh, 2022, p 265).

# Capacities of becoming and being: developing the student sense of 'self'

Students have a deep need to belong (Baumeister and Leary, 1995), to Be and Become someone in the world. Their life experiences also influence who they are, and being a student is what they 'do', as part of their identity and who they are. Siegel (2015) notes how the interplay and integration of mind, brain, body, and relationships enhances student health and well-being.

Baumeister (2011, p 48) notes the self is both *'utterly familiar, and yet surprisingly elusive'*. He suggests three basic root experiential elements to the self. First, students build an extensive and growing stock of knowledge about themselves: some true, some not, some known, yet much unknown. Second, the self is not simply within the body or the brain, it emerges, adapts, and modifies from interpersonal relations: the self is an interpersonal being. Third, the self is an agent, not just being, but also acting/doing. The self makes choices, regulates its responses and inner processes, and then initiates action, inherently to gain social acceptance (belonging/attachment/affiliation) (Baumeister, 2022). It is this becoming and being (see Wilcox, 1999), this transformation of the ontological self, that is said to be the wider purpose of Higher Education (Barnett, 2007). Barnett (2009, p 431) further examines the tension between knowing and being in a technological age where knowledge is readily accessible, arguing that elitist muddle-headedness *'lurks in the view that knowledge is "socially constructed", a view that often carries the silent "only" or "merely" before the "socially constructed"'.*

The self emerges and is experienced at the interface of the brain, body, and social system and is linked to identities, values, and belief systems. A coherent integrated self prevents the chaos which can arise and become an underlying cause of mental health issues. Student well-being is enhanced when their inside and outside world experiences utilise their natural capacities for experiencing and learning in an integrated and balanced way: this includes experiences of doing, sensing, thinking, feeling, and belonging, as a new Holistic Experiential Learning Theory proposed in this book.

Whilst human capacities generate specific aspects of an experience, they are continually integrated to form a complex flux. Picking up a cup by the top rim with your fingers, as mentioned earlier, is not experienced separately by each finger.

> ## Critical questions for practice
>
> » What kind of feelings do you want to engender in your work with students?
> » How could you develop a sense of belonging in your students?
> » How could you vary sensory experiences so that boredom doesn't set in?
> » What key thinking processes do you want to develop in your students?
> » How could you design experiences that facilitate voice, power, and agency to engender responsibility for learning?

The brain integrates to create a unified *whole* and so it is with learning. Models of learning should ideally acknowledge this experiencing complexity. In addition to their quotation earlier, Davis and Sumara reinforce the critical argument that the many capacities for experiencing (and learning) are operating in a continual state of interactive flux *'The focus of enquiry is not so much on the components (modes) of experience but, rather, on the relations that bind these elements together in action'* (1997, p 108).

Additional practical designs, that further translate the complexity of holistic experiential learning into everyday pedagogic practice, will be presented in the next chapter.

## Summary

- This chapter introduces the easy to remember holistic design model as a checklist to cover the seven significant student capacities for learning. The basics of design practice were introduced, such as working with design zones, route maps, the objectives-choreography dynamic, and other essential design principles.

- The 'errors of imagination' arising out of talking and writing were explored in terms of enhanced linguistic awareness and ways to reduce errors through the additional use of cognitive navigational tools derived from spatial metaphors and other linguistic forms. The concept of making student learning visible also helps reduce errors of imagination.

# Useful texts

Beard, C (2023) *Experiential Learning Design: Theoretical Foundations and Effective Principles.* New York: Routledge.

*This book offers a very comprehensive explanation of learning design, balancing the technical-rational with the artistic-choreography. The book highlights key theories with over 30 practical illustrations of experiential learning designs.*

Beard, C, Humberstone, B and Clayton, B (2014) Positive emotions: passionate scholarship and student transformation. *Teaching in Higher Education, 19*(6): 630–643.

*This paper challenges the practical and conceptual understanding of the role of emotions in Higher Education from the twin perspectives of transition and transformation. The research gives a good explanation of the neglected area of the positive emotions associated with learning.*

# Chapter 4 | Experiential learning design and creative practice

# Introduction

So far, design principles are founded on the notion that learning, when experiential, engages our exterior sensory capacities (exteroceptors) that link the student external world experiences (embedded) with the internal experiences (within the body, as embodied). Learning is relational (related to other actors), distributed (not residing in the mind of one individual), enacted (performed), and extended (beyond the body using ancillary 'tools' as extensions of the mind-body). In this chapter the principles of holistic design will be further explored in terms of everyday practical 'teaching' ideas, adding to the designs already introduced in previous chapters.

Learning experience design (LED) requires a two-fold approach: designing experiences '*for*' learning, interwoven with the design '*of*' learning. In the 1980s novel activities were introduced 'for' outdoor learning, including SAS style 'tough' adventure courses, driving tanks, making chocolates, juggling, drumming, and ready-made team-building kits to assemble. Articles later began to emerge questioning the extent of learning from experiences that focus on activity and novelty: one was titled: 'Still building rafts, juggling balls and driving tanks?' (Beard and Wilson, 2002). Interestingly, Kolb and his colleagues, in their research at US universities, were also concerned about the excessive focus on 'doing', on 'activity'. In the 1970s and 1980s, managers were thought to be spending insufficient time 'thinking' about what and why they were doing things in the way they did. Managers were regarded as stuck in an 'activity trap'. Kolb, a cognitive psychologist, recommended that managers spend more time on reflection. This raises the question as to whether other, more holistic approaches can be utilised to enhance learning to something other than post-activity reflection. Several designs now follow to offer alternative approaches to post-activity reflection.

Before progressing to show how holistic design principles can be embedded into everyday teaching, it might be helpful to summarise 12 design principles created so far in this and previous chapters.

1. 'Let the Learners Experience the Learning'.
2. Learning design: designing experiences 'for' learning (concrete experience/'activity') and designing experiences 'of' learning (integrating into the experience with an understanding of 'how students learn').
3. Draw three (or five) core design zones, such as beginning, middle, and end.
4. Create and add a learning journey map that functions as an outline for you and your students to follow. Maps existed before human speech and they can be used in many ways to support student learning. Use them to help you and your students to 'navigate' the journey.
5. Craft the outcomes and objectives.
6. Then add elements of creativity of choreography to generate a composition of experiences that will lead the students to arrive at the outcomes and objectives set.
7. A core concept to enable such creativity is 'deconstruction' – i.e. break things down like the parts of a jigsaw and then let the learners put it all back together.
8. The choreography requires the creation of shape and flow to the student learning experience. An example is the diamond shape that is the basis of a lot of meetings, in that they open up and after a specified time need to close down.
9. Consider the importance of space, and the ability to see relational and conceptual patterns usually relate to spatial thinking (spatial cognition).
10. Utilise the body (hands) to move (concrete) objects. These are called 'manipulatives' in mathematics (see the pedagogic literature on Object-Based Learning).
11. Utilise and engage the seven student capacities for learning where appropriate: doing, sensing, feelings, thinking, belonging in a social interactional sense, belonging in a more than human world sense, and being.
12. Design experiences that enhance memory.

**Figure 4.1** Summary of 12 core design principles

# Choreography

Ultimately objectives, traditionally knowledge-focused, are developed into a student learning experience. Choreography is a learning design process initiated by breaking down the objectives into smaller component parts. I use the term choreography because a person who crafts and coordinates sequences for films is referred to as a choreographer. Choreography is also a term associated with movement, dance, the stage, performance, and dramatic composition.

All living creatures, including humans, are animate, experiencing the world by moving in space. Humans live in a constant dynamic flux, a dance that emerges within the spatio-temporal world that surrounds us:

*A common kinetic thematic suffuses improvisational dance, human developmental life, and the lives of animate forms. In each case, a non-separation of thinking and doing is evident; so also is a non-separation of sensing and moving. In each case, qualities and presences are absorbed by a mindful body in the process of moving and thinking in movement.*

(Sheets-Johnstone, 2011, p 447)

The flow of thinking, moving, doing, and sensing forms the choreographic composition. The following design is an example of a process of deconstruction that helps create the elements of choreography.

## Example 4.1

### 'Word weaving' and the development of feedback and communication skills

In this example, the choreographic processes are initiated by breaking down topics, concepts, or terms located within the written objectives. All topics have keywords, and the unpacking of keywords can support the creative choreographic processes of learning design. Students are usually encouraged to define and discuss their terms in use, and they do this early on in their written assignments. Any word, or phrase, can be deconstructed to create a choreographic composition of an engaging learning experience. A seminar or lecture series might start with the question of *'what do we mean by x, y, or z?'*. For example, what do we mean by leadership, or what do we mean by psychology? I am going to take the word 'feedback' as an illustrative example.

The original design came about as a result of being commissioned to work with consultant anaesthetists in the UK to develop better feedback skills. I started the design process by asking the question: What do we mean by feedback, and what is good feedback? What I wanted to do was to create a learning experience whereby participants discussed their thoughts on these questions in some detail: the conversations were considered important in the design. This design has since been conducted with many groups of Higher Education students. The choreographic design process embraces the core principle: 'Let the learners experience the learning'. There are many sources of information on feedback, and (re-)searching is what we teach our students to do. Like any topic, there is usually a body of research in existence, and research literature can be explored in the deconstruction process. Details about the meaning of feedback can be found in textbooks, and research papers. Feedback will usually be defined in the Oxford dictionary, and AI software can also be consulted. By deconstructing the word 'feedback' and developing an answer to the question, What is good feedback?, an engaging learning experience can be created as follows.

The capacities for learning are harnessed during the reconstruction process, i.e. the construction of an answer to the question: What makes good feedback? This learning experience is called 'word weaving'; it allows learners to collectively weave the essential components of 'feedback' by working with packs of laminated cards with the following words on them:

Deficit, Development, Constructive, Critical, Feedback, Criticism, Judgments, Observations, Ideas, Answers, Feelings, Needs, Requests, Demands, Transmission, Transaction, Transformation, Destructive, Problem, Person, Subjective, Objective, Task, Process, Outcome, Solution, Problem, Opportunity, Intuition.

Three or four blank cards can be included to give the freedom to introduce additional words.

Groups of approximately four or five students place all the cards on the table, and a specified amount of time is allocated for students to construct a definition of good feedback. This process is not just a social construction process (i.e. conversational) as the body is used to move objects (cards) in space (spatial cognition) to construct sentences that form their answer to the question. The students not only have conversations, they also select and eliminate cards, and sequence words, through collaborative decision making. The students capture their final thoughts and capture their answers with recordings (capturing). Being told they will hear the work of highly skilled anaesthetists creates a sense of competition and high levels of student engagement. Several live recordings of student definitions of feedback have been recorded, and two excellent constructions of definitions of good feedback by the consultant anaesthetists are shown next:

1. Feedback necessarily evokes feelings as it involves a series of observations which may be a subjective analysis of performance, often, but not always, involving judgement (implied or inferred). It is an opportunity to identify problems or deficits to help people generate their own ideas and answers in order to transform their practice, change their behaviour, and solve problems.

2. Feedback is an ongoing process that acknowledges the feelings and needs of both parties. Feedback is based on direct observation, and objectives, and represents an opportunity to share ideas for development. It should not be based solely on deficits, or problems, rather it should be part of a series of transactions that aim for a transformation of that person, that both parties have carefully reflected on.

Here we see a clear distinction between instruction and experiential learning design. The design of the experience of learning takes centre-stage, and the student gains 'acquaintance with' rather than just 'knowledge of' the subject or topic. The depth of understanding is enhanced by collaborative questioning and group discussion during the construction process. I have a handout with an AI-generated answer that turns out to be very similar to those just mentioned: simply giving this information (knowledge) would not generate any depth of understanding, as the knowledge on the handout is quickly forgotten. Definitions of good feedback from participants can be developed further as future cohorts can inherit the earlier ideas. Whilst the design process outlined earlier involves words, other examples will follow to illustrate how images, or real or simulated objects, can be used.

The next practical example illustrates 'container theory', a concept of a space 'containing' types. They belong 'in' a specific place because they are typical of that category. This concept is important for many disciplines, especially for botany and zoology. Animals and plants are classified into types, and this can be quite complex to learn that classification of Kingdom, Phyla, Class, Order, Family, Genera, Species, and Sub-species.

This design uses a real container, with real objects, but the objects are not complex animate creatures. Careful observation, hand manipulation, and discussion are used to develop learning. This simulation design can be used to create an initial understanding of the core classification principles.

# Example 4.2

## Classification: nuts and bolts and animate beings

This design develops the ability to carefully examine a set of objects. The experience replicates some of the observational skills required for zoologists and botanists, though general category classification occurs in many other disciplines. Sets of small plastic containers with screw lids were used to contain what are known as 'fixtures and fittings', including assorted nails, screws, nuts and bolts, raw plugs, and washers. These function as 'concrete objects' to be manipulated by the hands/body, to assess form (what can be seen, what they look like) which implies specific functions (how they work). Collaborative inquiry occurs through the sharing of ideas in the small group settings. Using large flipchart paper laid flat on the desk, the student groups each create a hierarchical analysis chart by drawing lines between objects to show their groupings, or types. The details of what makes a screw different from a nail, and a bolt different from a nail, for example, requires observation and description to identify separate characteristics. The end point is to produce a classification chart that can be used by anyone to establish how these items can be separated, classified, and named based on their form and function. The chart makes student learning visible.

Eco-linguistics, as a form of critical discourse analysis, emerged in the 1990s as a new paradigm of linguistic research, when sociolinguistics was widened to include not only the social context in which language is embedded, but also to incorporate the broader, more ecological context. Eco-linguistics can be utilised to reveal how the stories we live by subconsciously underpin unsustainable practices in society. The practical example (example 4.3) describes a relatively simple pedagogic design that applies eco-linguistic analysis (Stibbe, 2021) to foster a critical awareness in students of the way that eco-tourism language might consciously or subconsciously endorse unsustainable societies.

## Example 4.3

### 'Reading' text: critical discourse analysis

Students are asked to read and analyse images and text, including titles and sub-titles. The sources for reading were laid out on a table to allow choice, to take copies, and to return to select others for further analysis. Initially, reading requires a quiet solo experience, followed by a final group analysis. All the articles, taken from weekend newspapers, were focused on wildlife, and most were located in the tourism section. The central question for the students to answer was: How is wildlife portrayed in the popular weekend press? The overarching findings of students from across the globe is captured in the following text:

The articles have references to 'eye catching', commercialised narratives that draw reader attention by emphasising big, ugly, rare, and ferocious animals. Typically, the emphasis is on large and popular, high-profile mammals, such as the big cats, hippos, rhinos, buffaloes, and wild dogs. Wildlife is frequently portrayed as fashionable to see, almost a league table 'must see' approach, with sought after, prized 'tick list collections', or trophies. The narrative focus is often centred on adventure, danger, and fear, of the exclusive or exotic, or as wildlife existing as commodities for human entertainment. Whilst mammals, birds, and sharks were frequent subjects for these stories, smaller animals, and plants, were rarely included in eco-tourism narratives. The prominence of anthropomorphic branding language in eco-tourism narratives is typified by flamingos for example being portrayed as 'exquisitely pointless' creatures, as victims of fashion, flying in huge flocks not unlike a 'giant pink duvet'.

The analysis of these eco-tourism narratives was carried out many times by both UK and international Higher Education students, including doctoral students. They concluded that these anthropocentric narratives portray nature as: for human consumption and entertainment; predominantly high-profile mammals that are eye catching, big, rare, ugly, scary, and fierce. Plants and smaller living creatures were portrayed as insignificant, with some creatures referred to as 'pointless'. The participants generally agreed that future tourism researchers should utilise eco-linguistic analysis to help them to identify opportunities to change the tourism narratives, to promote a broad shift from ego-centric to eco-centric approach. These readings exposed a set of specific semantic characteristics that create negative stereotypical representations of the natural world. The predominant metaphors, located within the depictive and descriptive formats, use human, ego-centric, as opposed to eco-centric narratives that are recommended in the 2030 Tourism Sustainable Development Goals.

One significant outcome of this eco-linguistic design was the co-production (students and myself), of my chapter on Wildlife Adventure Tourism in the world's first book on Adventure Tourism (Swarbrooke et al., 2003).

The development of writing skills and associated analytical processes, as highlighted earlier, can also be designed as a 'live' experience. Using student-tutor collaboration and co-construction, good writing skills can be developed using speech recognition technology to create a shared on-screen learning experience. The 'production' of a student-tutor generated digital handout creates focus. I call this design 'live crafting'.

# Reducing errors of imagination

In *Thinking Visually*, Stephen Reed (2022, p 3) notes that *'Language is a marvelous tool for communication, but it is generally overrated as a tool for thought'*. As mentioned earlier, written and spoken words take a linear form, and so it is hard to speak or write about a complex multi-dimensional concept. Thus, when learners read or listen to the words of a teacher, the learner imagines what it is that the teacher is trying to create in the mind, and this often leads to 'errors of imagination' that are invisible to the teacher. This is why people often say that they read a book but when they went to see the film it was not what they imagined.

These errors of imagination can be reduced by raising self-awareness of the linguistic metaphors used in speaking or writing. These metaphors are usually related to sensory, bodily, or spatial form and they are designed as scaffolding to help the brain understand and imagine phenomena. Let me give some spatial examples: those two people seem *close*; I work in Higher Education; there are also institutions called *Further* Education; you have your life *in front* of you; that category *contains* all those with; I think it best to put that *behind* you. There are also numerous up-down metaphors, such as: it is important to step *up* to the new level; feeling *down*; an all-time low; things are looking up. These spatial or bodily metaphors offer additional ways to deconstruct written objectives to aid the choreographic processes. Metaphors create additional cognitive scaffolding that helps improve thinking and conceptual understanding, and learning can be enhanced by scaffolding, in the form of objects, arrows, pictures, animations, icons, etc.

# Critical issues

## Codes and complexity

Two codes will now be introduced to augment the understanding of the need for a holistic pedagogy. The first code is B.C.H.S.Ec, which represents the dominant historical paradigms over time concerning the changes in understanding of how humans learn (see Beard & Wilson, 2018). The code is: Behaviouralism, Cognitivism, Humanism and Social constructivism; the final code Ec represents an emerging Ecological complexity, which recognises that all these major paradigms play an important role in learning, and that learning exists within a complex flux of connectivity (see also Barnett, 2018). Experiential designs will need to embrace pedagogic complexity in the 21st century. A complex design example is described in chapter 5.

The 'reading' and 'unpacking' of text is a common practice in Higher Education. Whilst the 'reading' of text is often taken literally, here I introduce the critical questions of 'what' is being read, and 'how' this reading occurs. Many of the examples illustrated so far include the use of hands to 'read', and write, and to manipulate, feel, sense, touch, and move things. So why do we neglect the role of the hands in learning? Can the hands learn? The second code, H.D.O.A.C., addresses this question. It stands for learning by handling, discussing, organising (spatial complexity), analysing (spatial patterns), and conceptualising (abstract thinking). This is a more holistic approach compared to post-experience reflection proposed by Kolb (1984). I have observed, over many years, that when students are presented with objects to support their learning, the first thing they do is to pick the objects up, and, in an inquisitive way, manipulate them with their hands. Why is this so? The students appear to be using their hands to 'read' the objects. To use a bodily metaphor they gain 'first-*hand*' experience of them.

The following practical example, concerning the emergence of an Industrial Ecology (also called the Circular Economy), highlights a design of a particularly complex topic. The Industrial Ecology experience applies the previously mentioned code, H.D.O.A.C, to guide the sequence of student actions, moving from object manipulation with the hands (H) through to abstract conceptualisation (C). Arrows are also used to highlight relational (spatial) patterns: the code and arrows are scaffolding tools used to raise student awareness of important learning processes. In this design the objects are used as 'manipulatives'; the hand moves and manipulates objects, and this is a powerful way to enhance understanding. It is interesting that *'the hand and the mouth require more brain power than any other body parts'* (Lundborg, 2014, p 89). When people see objects, the brain automatically activates plans for actions that they could perform on or with these objects. Neuropsychological research suggests that when objects with strong associations to possible actions, such as tools, pre-motor and motor areas of the brain are activated. People experience greater motor activation when viewing objects that are readily manipulatable, as opposed to viewing objects that are not readily available to be manipulated. These findings suggest that when people see particular objects, they perceive affordances from actions on those objects (see Macrine and Fugate, 2022).

The experience design in example 4.4 highlights hand manipulation in a wide range of objects that are readily available for purchase, all of which convey specific information about the underlying principles of the emerging Industrial Ecology.

## Example 4.4

### The concept of an 'Industrial Ecology'

A core textbook on Industrial Ecology (Bourg and Erkman, 2003) contains a description on the back of the book to describe the key concepts of Industrial Ecology. In the design of this learning experience it is important to try and highlight these patterns and to encourage the students to reproduce them by showing these conceptual ideas using a range of commercial products. Labels can be provided for students to place next to their highlighted concepts, as an additional way to make conceptual thinking more visible.

Business as usual in terms of industrial and technological development – even if based on a growing fear of pollution and shortages of natural resources – will never deliver sustainable development. However, the growing interest in recent years in the new science of industrial ecology (IE), and the idea that industrial systems should *mimic quasi-cyclical functions of natural ecosystems* and 'industrial food *chain*', holds promise in addressing not only short-term environmental problems but also the long-term holistic *evolution of industrial systems*. This possibility requires a number of key conditions to be met, not least the restructuring of our manufacturing and consumer society to *reduce* the effects of *material and energy flows* at the very point in history when globalisation is rapidly increasing them. The *systematic recovery* of industrial wastes, the minimisation of losses caused by dispersion, the *dematerialisation* of the economy, the requirement to decrease our reliance on fuels derived from hydrocarbons, etc. (Note: Italicised words have been added to highlight the deconstruction process used in the choreography of the design).

The products are divided into four areas and placed in four different small bags for four groups to work with. The areas covered by each bag are (1) technology; (2) everyday domestic products; (3) materials; and (4) products produced by artists. In each bag there are five plastic cards each with one letter on to create a guiding code: H.D.O.A.C. (handle, discuss, organise, analyse, conceptualise). This provides a sequence for students to follow to move from practical handling to the creation of abstract conceptualisation of the key concepts of Industrial Ecology. The code H.D.O.A.C. offers a comprehensive and inclusive approach to learning: it is more complex than the cognitive focus on post-experience reflection suggested by Kolb (1984).

The code sequence encourages students to focus on a range of human capacities such as sensory-motor manipulation of objects by the body (especially the hands), social interaction, pattern detection using spatial cognition, and finally high-level abstract conceptualisation. In this experience the students initially, and naturally, manipulate the objects with their hands. This is important as the process activates sensory-motor areas of the brain, and this can lead to enhanced episodic memories. Taking one key word, *dematerialisation*, the products can highlight this principle in many ways. Two examples found in the product bags are as follows.

(1) In the technology bag there are examples of plastic cards that have various technological capacities built into them, such as the key card used in hotels. Within the same bag there is also a metal key. When students place an arrow between these two objects they will *see* the relationship between the two. The metal key has less flexibility and requires the consumption of a lot more energy and use of precious materials in its manufacture and use for a physical door lock. Unlocking a door is the only function of the metal key. Plastic or wooden cards are recyclable, and they can be digitally reprogrammed and reused: they are a 'phygital' product, combining the physical material with a digital component. These changes all point to a reduction in physical material use, and so is an example of dematerialisation.

(2) The technology bag also contains a smart phone. The smart phone of course contains a torch, a calculator, an alarm clock, maps, dictation recording devices, and many other apps that are capable of many functions. The smart phone reduces the need to carry all these items, and there is a considerable reduction of material use, and material loss. The production of all these separate items would entail the consumption of a lot of resources/materials. The smart phone can be shown with arrows radiating out in a circular fashion to show how many other products are not required as separate items as they are incorporated within the smart phone device. The smart phone is a prime example of a multi-functional device that exhibits the concept of dematerialisation.

(3) Third, the technology bag also contains a very small, but powerful, human energy powered torch. It is a wind-up torch, but the reason it is powerful is that it uses LED bulbs. Larger torches that used old incandescent bulbs were much bigger, and therefore required much more material to make them. They also consumed more energy to produce less light. Incandescent bulbs consume energy that results in 97% heat, and 3% light.

As can be seen in the examples so far, high levels of student engagement and observational skills are naturally generated through intentional design. The following example focuses on the observational skills required to develop an ability to 'read' (in an academic sense), descriptive (text), and depictive (images) form.

Multi-media research concentrates on the principles of how people learn through the building of mental representations derived from words (spoken or printed text) and pictures (e.g. photos, maps, video, or animation). The foundational multi-media theory is known as 'Dual Coding Theory' (see Sadoski and Paivio, 2013), which suggests two distinct cognitive processing channels: one for visual imagery (depictive form) and one specialised for processing words and text (descriptive form). This may be a limited perspective: it is likely there are many cognitive processing 'channels'. In a chapter titled 'Games as multi-sensory experiences', Nicola Whitton discusses a wide range of multi-media principles that are concerned with core sensory experiences, and she points out the limitations of the idea of just text and visuals. Whitton comments that '*modern digital games employ an array of media types, including visual elements, animations, cut scenes and video, text, speech, sound effects and music*' (Whitton, 2014, p 169). In addition, the evolving haptic interface adds gesture-touch and vibration capacities to enhance online learning experience.

## Summary

- Time spent on experience design is critical, more so than designing for delivery. The processes of deconstruction were explored as a way of breaking topics down into their component parts, to create the foundations for choreographic design. Deconstruction generates a sequence of simple stages that are used to get started with the design process.

- Practical examples were introduced in this chapter to examine the way that increased complexity can be embraced in holistic learning designs for students.

- This chapter also explored practical ways to enhance navigational and observational skills, spatial cognition, the role of objects as manipulatives, the use of the hands in corporeal-kinaesthetic learning, by presenting six brief illustrations that show 'design in practice'. They each highlight different ways to improve student engagement, by harnessing their learning capacities in ways that enhance memory. The examples all highlight aspects of choreography. Choreography helps with the more artistic aspects of experience design, providing a design link between the art and creativity, with the science of planning and objective setting.

- When delivery involves a live experience, such as live crafting for developing student writing skills, the outcome is less predictable, and so can be perceived as having more risk for tutors.

# Useful texts

Denis, M (2018) *Space and Spatial Cognition: A Multi-disciplinary Perspective.* Oxon: Routledge.

*This book is concerned with space and spatial knowledge, and it highlights how important space is in terms of learning, conceptual thinking, and the mental capacities we utilise to represent the spatial world we inhabit.*

Stibbe, A (2021) *Ecolinguistics: Language, Ecology and the Stories We Live By.* Oxon: Routledge.

*This book is especially useful for understanding critical discourse analysis, and, in particular, the specific practical example 4.4 on eco-linguistics. The book is also useful in a general sense in that it helps in understanding how language shapes the world we live in, and how subtle linguistics influences, conceals, promotes, or inhibits thinking.*

# Chapter 5 | Complex designs for experiential learning

## Introduction

This chapter further develops the notion of learning design complexity by presenting a detailed analysis of two contrasting designs. One is a redesign of a level 4 (first year) module that took about 80 hours to create a new design, prepare new materials, and allow time for staff buy-in as the seminars were delivered by a large teaching team. The second design, at level 7 (postgraduate), took nearly 15 years to evolve through a continuous process of choreography to the point where the module became extremely successful, producing high levels of engagement and achievement. This design facilitated an understanding of the more complex designs.

The first-year example exposes how previous student perceptions of the module, along with poor design and redesign, contributed to low levels of attendance and low achievement. The module redesign suffered from the politics of participating disciplines, which, along with multiple demands from senior managers, generated negative energy. For a new design to succeed, a detailed understanding of these underlying issues had to be acknowledged and opened-up for discussion. This example highlights how design can never be divorced from the wider context.

## The problem of 'teaching' applied academic skills at level 4

This redesign reflects a classic problem that many universities face, notably the resistance and gradual disengagement of students with specific modules that are (ironically) designed to support the development of academic and personal and professional skills. Over a period of approximately 30 years, this module faced considerable student resistance. Historically there had been many iterations of this module, with different titles such as 'Flying Start' and 'Personal and Professional Development': all suffered from low levels of success.

One of the problems the module faced included the many attempts to redesign through a process of competing conversations about what to try next in formal meetings, rather than using design principles and a collective 'drawing board'. Tensions occurred between managers and teaching teams about content (for example about the balance of employability skills such as teamworking and communication; portfolios, self-assessment, IT skills; and academic writing and referencing skills). Further tensions surfaced amongst subject teams over the degree to which their subject was to be accommodated in the design of this generic first year module. The result was a disconnected and disjointed module that lacked coherence.

In September 2023 it once again became very clear that the module wasn't working and that a more dramatic change was needed. I offered to lead the redesign of this module as an experiential approach. In truth I was the only member of staff offering to help as others had lost the appetite to attempt yet another iteration. The situation was made worse by the fact that no workload hours were allocated for redesign due to financial pressures. This reinforces my comment in chapter 1 about design neglect and the need for change in work-loading practices. The cost of 30 years of lack of success was considerable, not least in terms of the wider impact on the student experience.

First, middle managers made a game changing decision by agreeing to have this module delivered as a four-week 'block teaching' intense experience to support the student transition into Higher Education. This meant that this was to be the only module that the first-year students experienced in the first four weeks. The block teaching approach was to include the five service-sector subject areas of Hospitality, Food and Nutrition, Tourism, Events, and Airline Management. Staff buy-in was important and necessary.

The next difficult question related to 'teaching' versus designing a very different 'experience' for the students. I dedicated design time during the summer by extending my stay in a hotel for three days after attending an Educational Excellence Board meeting with an apprenticeship company. This retreat allowed for focused concentration on a new design, and my decision to donate time to do this design to the best of my ability occurred as a positive gesture in my last year before retiring.

With the help of the module leader, and support from some of the more experienced staff in the academic teams, we tried to understand the reasons why the students perceived the module as unnecessary: review data suggested that the module was seen as divorced from the student core studies. We decided it was time to be brave and change a lot of things. But we needed to get staff buy-in first. Example 5.1 briefly explains seven design changes.

## Example 5.1

### The design of a level 4 module

1.  **Seminars were designed to 'Let the Learners Experience the Learning'**, and a clear module 'shape and flow' was created for the overall module and for each seminar and lecture. All designs had a clear, functional beginning, middle, and end. Academic, and personal and professional, skills were designed to be more acceptable: they were carefully interwoven, camouflaged, and disguised within this core subject generic critical question. The design emphasised continuous assignment support through the seminars, in a way that built confidence. The assignment was to be constructed built in a co-creative way in stages during the seminars, like a jigsaw, to increase attendance. Staff and students were to co-construct a repository of articles and books to share.

2.  **We changed the assessment to create more connectivity with the student core studies so that the module did not appear as solely academic skills development such as writing and referencing.** There was also a new focus on how to complete the assignment with staff providing support, using a constructivist approach so staff and students worked together to create aspects of the thinking and writing-up as the module progressed. The core assignment question was broad yet complex: *What do we mean by the term 'experience'?* This was seen by students as more clearly linked to their core studies (five service-sector subject areas of Hospitality, Food and Nutrition, Tourism, Events, and Airline Management).

3.  **We changed the way the module was 'taught' by academic staff.** The module was designed so that it was more student and experience centred in the design approach. Peer relation building was given extra attention, and lecturers played an important role in supporting the student sense of belonging. A room with whiteboards all round was used to take staff on the module visual 'journey' so that they could see the flow of the whole four-week design. The design was such that there was more flexibility for staff to cater for the subject specialisms. Early on staff were encouraged to clearly express either buy-in or concerns about these design ideas.

4.  **The module design was given an increased financial investment so that all the subject centres could provide short 'experiential' field trips.**

5.  **We introduced comprehensive learning route maps** (introduced in chapter 3) for all seminars and lectures to highlight their module four-week journey, as a navigational support tool. The icon – *'You are here'* – was moved for each lecture or seminar to enable students to 'locate' where they were in their journey, and allow students to look back, and look forward.

6. **Lecture material was posted online as a PDF file.** The use of a PDF was to emphasise the incentives of attending the 'live' experience. Attending was presented as the better option if students were to get the best experience. PDF files had no animations. New resources and references were introduced in each live seminar session.

7. **We included and spoke about important experiences that might affect the students' mental health and well-being (see chapter 6)**, such as issues associated with moving on from adolescence to adulthood. The design introduced the OK Corral Life Positions (Transactional Analysis), mental health and addictive behaviours, the way that the unconscious mind controls the brain, etc. These issues were presented as part of the assessment question: *What do we mean by the term 'experience'?* The students were asked what gave them pleasure during this module learning experience as positive emotions in learning are rarely spoken about.

*The result*

Space only allows for a brief statement of the results. Module teaching teams' response was overwhelmingly positive, with most saying that the module teaching was very enjoyable. The student Module Evaluation Questionnaires were good, the attendance increased, and there were relatively few students who failed to attend most of the sessions. The module leader was pleased with the results. The new design now forms a strong design template to build on for the future.

## Critical questions for practice

» Who takes responsibility for the design of the 'whole' experience?

» What problems arise when specific staff take responsibility for specific parts of the student learning experience?

## Critical issues

The description of this first-year redesign raises some important issues. Whilst 12 generic design principles are shown in chapter 4, this design highlights how specific contextual elements cannot be ignored. Good design is not sufficient in terms of success. There are usually multiple stakeholders that can influence the outcome. Accommodating the wishes of these stakeholders must be a negotiated process within the overall design.

> This example highlights how a combination of contextual elements have to be taken into account in the final design: political and cultural context, power relations between management and academic staff, competing design ideas, tensions between disciplines, student perceptions of modules and subsequent resistance to specific types of generic support. These processes are all time consuming, adding to the general lack of recognition of design as a time-consuming process.

The next design example at the postgraduate level is called 'Walk-the-Talk'. It outlines several important principles in the creation of more complex, long-term learning design. This example involves an initial new design, followed by years of continuous improvement, redesign, and long-term planning. This design approach highlights a specific beginning design with a focus on power, relationship building, and the development of an active co-creative process of engagement and discovery learning.

This design was initially conceived and delivered as an adult evening class experience commissioned by the UK Workers Education Association in my role as the Conservation Director of the Staffordshire Wildlife Trust. The class was delivered in a local community that wanted to be more actively involved in environmental issues, including local planning issues. After three years of delivery the original design was developed for use at university where it was taught to mature students studying a postgraduate module.

In terms of long-term design, the vision was that many learning materials had to be co-created by students (Let the students do the learning). These could then be made available across several cohorts over time, i.e. the creation of a process of what is called 'inheritance' (of materials and resources).

## Example 5.2

### A 'Walk-the-Talk' design at level 7

This level 7 design was my sole responsibility to design and teach. What follows is a descriptive outline of a postgraduate learning experience design that utilises many student core capacities for learning. The topic in this example was 'The Evolution of the UK Environmental Movement', which included, for example, the understanding of the voluntary NGOs and their tactics, environmental and related laws, significant events, key milestones, animal and plant extinctions, environmental disasters, contributions by specific individuals, and the diverse involvement of private and public organisations.

The design involved the creation of three distinct phases, each with a very different learning experience in terms of the way that students interact with knowledge, peers, objects, and materials. The students work together in small groups during these three phases. The first phase involved acquiring information about a specific chosen topic area such as: when certain organisations were established; which government bodies were set up, when, and why; and the impact that specific environmental events had on development and change, etc. This initial phase, involving fact-finding, is termed the 'Informational Phase'. In this early phase substantial amounts of basic information are acquired by multiple student groups, then shared, and discussed among the wider student cohort before progressing to the next stage. Production is an important principle in design: this can take the form of a range of documents, including booklets, databases, and book reviews. These become foundational material for future cohorts to inherit, who can then further develop and update these each year.

Over several years complex student databases, covering several hundred years of the evolution of the environmental movement, can be co-constructed in digital and paper formats for further analysis. This 'Information Phase' serves other additional purposes, such as the development of a sense of confidence (affective domain); a responsibility for learning; a sense of belonging to, and interdependence with, peers and the lecturer. This phase was in preparation for, and a prerequisite to move to, the next, more complex, phase: knowledge acquisition generates only a limited understanding, which is sometimes referred to as 'surface learning' (Marton and Säljö, 1976), and so the second phase experience, called the 'Relational Phase', explores connections and relationships between the complex mass of collected information.

During the second phase students are required to develop a greater depth of understanding, beyond knowledge acquisition. This phase works with the many facts and figures, and details of events and other information, to develop an evolutionary narrative about the environmental movement. The core output in this phase is a physical representation created by students to represent the spatial-relational complexity of interrelated events. The representation of this complexity took the form of a large floor map, not unlike the iconic cartography in the London Underground Map design. As each group lays out their own specific contribution on the floor map, their learning is made visible to the lecturer by using colour-coded laminated cards with key dates and other information on. When the other groups add their own specific research topic information, a shared collective representation develops that possesses a time and space 'fit' (see Kirsh, 2010). This skeletal but complex representation acts as a visual tool (see Verschaffel et al., 2010) to be explored and further developed in a process that enhances thinking and reasoning. By making visible the complex evolutionary narrative, the students interact by walking among the cards (bodily/sensory capacities as embodied), critically examining the map from different spatial and temporal perspectives, and articulating (oral) and sharing (social) what they see (sensory/observation/thinking aloud).

As relational complexity emerges, reflective conversations generate a depth of understanding (higher abstract conceptualisation) of the evolution of the environmental movement, which then generates further queries and questions. This Walk-the-Talk experience can be recorded, captured, and posted online to be digitally shared for further analysis, including comments and challenging questions from the lecturer.

The third and final phase, termed the 'Transformation Phase', involves a higher level of critical reflection, dissonance, and discomfort, where values, beliefs, views, and existing interpretations are challenged and questioned. Questions included: What is the political story behind this spatially expanded timeline? Why are the leading characters mostly Western men? In what ways has the voluntary movement developed or been thwarted in terms of their tactics over periods of time? What is your own personal contribution to environmental change?

# Design complexity

Whilst the full extent of the postgraduate design example cannot be presented here, a full paper has been published in *Reflective Practice* (Beard, 2018). The title is: 'Learning Experience Designs (LEDs) in an age of complexity: time to replace the lightbulb'. The paper highlights how research from a range of disciplines can be utilised to develop a very complex learning experience design that embraces several modes of experiencing located in the Holistic Experiential Learning Theory. The paper explores the incorporation of active *doing* (e.g. producing databases, booklets, and fact sheets), *sensing* (e.g. moving colour-coded cards containing key facts with their hands to place them in the correct spatial and temporal relationship in a way that produces a pictorial and textual representation of the evolutionary narratives), *thinking* (e.g. developing abstract reasoning through discussion), and *belonging* (e.g. engaging in a variety of peer interactions). The students also experience and share a range of *feelings* during the three phases (the joys of sharing and self-discovery, the unsettling feelings that are the result of dissonance created by the design of difficult questioning that challenges the assumptions held by the group or individuals). In practice all the core learning capacities are interactively intertwined in a complex experiential fluidity, and an important design skill is the ability to understand how the experiences are put together, to create the overarching shape and flow of the 'whole' experience (see Beard, 2023).

## Summary

- This chapter explores two very different designs at two different levels of a university education. They each highlight different design issues. The first example came about due to successive module design failures that resulted in low levels of attendance, and low levels of engagement. The political context is highlighted as an influencing force in design.

- The second presents a more complex design, highlighting how different phases of learning can be introduced and made visible during a module. The three distinct beginning, middle, and end phases of design occur within a wider design that has an overall shape and flow. This design has considerable theoretical depth, using research from many fields and disciplines. In each phase students interact with peers, lecturers, and module materials in very different ways. This example also highlights a co-creation process in practice as part of a longer-term vision of students producing resources for themselves and for future cohorts (inheritance).

## Useful texts

Beard, C (2018) Learning Experience Designs (LEDs) in an age of complexity: time to replace the lightbulb. *Reflective Practice*, *19*(6): 736–748.

*This paper is a detailed published account of the second design example presented earlier. The paper highlights the considerable theoretical depth that underpins a continuous process of redesign.*

Sheets-Johnstone, M (2009) *The Corporeal Turn: An Interdisciplinary Reader*. Exeter, UK: Imprint Academic.

*There is no better advocate for the role of the body in learning than Maxine Sheets-Johnstone. In an age when the brain dominates much discourse, and at a time when the term 'neuro' is a prefix for many fields of study, then this book places the bodily capacities to learn back at centre-stage to redress the balance in mind-body debates.*

# Chapter 6 | Learning experience designs to enhance well-*being*

# Introduction

In this chapter I will highlight how the Holistic Experiential Learning Theory (HELT) has potential to provide a platform for enhancing student mental health and well-being which is a major concern for universities. Jones et al. (2023, p 60) report that '*Rates of mental health problems in undergraduates are prevalent on a global scale*'. They offer a short but comprehensive analysis of some of the key literature in their book, *Transition into Higher Education*. The transition period from school to university is known to be an area of concern, partly because there are financial consequences related to retention and progression data monitoring by funding authorities.

Sensitivity, stigma, and isolation associated with admitting to having mental health issues is evident in comments by Jones et al. (2023, p 63) about students appreciating '*access to an online app without anyone knowing that they need support*'. Other comments refer to students finding it '*useful to understand that the feelings they were experiencing through the first year were quite normal*'. Although mental health is being addressed in universities, particularly by Student Support Services, the connection between learning and well-being has been neglected, or misunderstood.

This chapter focuses on the development of higher levels of student consciousness and awareness concerning (1) the processes of learning about their learning experiences and (2) the transformative impact on life that this awareness can bring as a result of well-designed learning experiences. The brain is sculpted by experience, and success in life depends on the ability to learn-to-learn from experience: Moon (2004, p 104) argues that '*all learning is, in effect, learning from experience*'. In the 'attention economy', much of what we attend to is harvested and monetised: adjusting our mode of attention can have far-reaching and quite profound effects: being observant as to how we observe alters what we observe (see McGilchrist, 2019).

In *Learning to Learn from Experience*, Cell (1984, p viii) compares what he understands as academic learning, with experiential learning, the latter being defined as:

*learning in which the learner is directly in touch with the realities being studied. It is contrasted with learning which the learner only reads about, only hears about, talks about, or writes about these realities but never comes into contact with them as part of the learning process.*

These notions of 'being in touch with' and 'coming into contact with' what is being studied appear to be central to the way that Cell understands experiential learning. Cell suggests that 'academic' learning only focuses on talking, reading, and writing. These are unhelpful dualisms, when traditional academic approaches to teaching are not considered as learning experiences within a broader ecology of learning experiences. The extent to which 20th century, traditional 'instructional' methods are being used to disseminate knowledge and skills remains the subject of much discussion. For teachers it is certainly not an easy task to embrace the complexities of learning design in ways that allow students to experience becoming 'acquainted with' their subject. Lectures and seminars in universities do focus on factual content, though this tends to involve content delivery through a process of construction, mostly using social interaction, with slides, containing a combination of text and images to aid the process.

The focus of teaching design in Higher Education should ideally be three-fold, about what needs to be learned, how to learn, and how to learn how to learn. The latter involves a raising of awareness, and a bringing-into-consciousness the capacities to learn and develop for life. The beginning, middle, and end design zones present different opportunities to focus on mental health and well-being. Caine and Caine (1994, p 116) advocate making the core elements of experience visible, arguing that *'educators need to identify and appreciate the various elements of experience and need to know how to bring them together effectively'*. A strong focus on the HELT presents greater potential to bring into awareness the whole student being in ways that can develop flourishing and well-being by developing an integrated and balanced self. A disconnect with the self means losing touch with thoughts, feelings, the sensing body, and one's beliefs and values.

## Critical questions for practice

» Who controls what happens in both the physical and digital classroom?

» In what ways can mental health and well-being be connected to the processes of learning to learn in Higher Education?

» It is said that Higher Education transforms lives: in what way does this happen?

In their book, *Nurturing the Whole Student: Five Dimensions of Teaching and Learning*, Mayes and Williams (2013) suggest the dimensions that are the foundations of holistic learning are organic, psychodynamic, affiliative, procedural, and existential: this has resonance with the HELT. Their term organic suggests that learning is embodied, involving learning by sensing and doing, by utilising a neural network that is not solely within the head but extended out into the whole body. Their term psychodynamic includes working with student emotions and feelings related to student behaviours that result from past conflicts, whilst the term affiliative recognises the existence of a deep human need to belong, to develop secure attachments and affiliations with others. Their fourth dimension, procedural, alludes to the processes of learning, and is described as a cognitive apprenticeship to increase awareness of the cognitive processes of critical thinking and knowing. Finally, their fifth dimension is existential. This existential self I refer to as being, though for much of the lives of students, and teachers, consists of a journey of becoming. These five dimensions align with the HELT (Beard, 2023) and design modelling.

It is not easy to increase the student awareness of the way that learning can positively influence their inner and outer life experiences in ways that improve their mental

## Critical issues

### Transformation of the *self* in Higher Education

Many Higher Education institutions make claims to 'transform lives', and this is the marketing strapline of my university. Long ago Barnett suggested that approaches to student learning should pay attention to the wider purpose of Higher Education, which he argued was not the development of the epistemological self, but rather the development of the ontological self (Barnett, 2007). It is this notion of the 'ontological self', of the student being, that aligns with the fifth existential dimension proposed by Mayes and Williams. If universities are to pay greater attention to the transformation of the ontological self, this requires much greater awareness, a noticing, and a bringing into consciousness of student capacities to experience the world, including an understanding of the ways that experience influences the development of the mind. This is the essence of experiential learning. Heightening the consciousness of the experience of learning has potential to create profound transformation.

health and well-*being*. In earlier chapters I have quoted Lakoff and Nunez (2000, p 1) as saying that '*most of the brain is devoted to vision, motion, spatial understanding, interpersonal interaction, coordination, emotions, language, and everyday reasoning*'. If these eight areas represent the *experiencing* focus of the brain, then they offer a good starting point for areas to increase student awareness.

Siegel notes how '*The mind is using the brain to create itself*' (2007, p 32); this is significant as he is making it clear that the student learning experience will shape and reshape their neural wiring in a positive way when higher levels of self-awareness are developed, preventing the subconscious mind from controlling much of what students think, do, sense, feel, and become. The idea of life as a very personal, partially developed film with an incomplete script that each person writes is a powerful metaphor.

Low level self-awareness arises from the chaos and rigidity of a non-integrated self, when the self is controlled by the subconscious. This can lead to negative feelings, and negative behaviours. It is important to find space and time when 'teaching' to inform students of these issues and offer basic down-to-earth advice on mental health issues within everyday teaching. The wise words of the Chinese philosopher Lao Tzu suggest that we should be careful about our *thoughts*, which can be turned into *words*, and our *words* turned into *actions*, and our *actions* turned into *habits*. Our *habits* in turn embed themselves within our *character*, contributing towards our *being*, and our destiny. This ancient philosophical aphorism highlights the need to be careful, to become more aware and conscious of the complex inter-relationship between thinking, speaking, agency and behaviour, character development, belonging, becoming, and being. Lao Tzu points to the need for a greater consciousness to avoid the mind being (often unconsciously) influenced, conditioned, and controlled by past experiences.

## Example 6.1

### Experience and the conditioned self

To illustrate the philosophical perspective by Lao Tzu about being aware and careful of our thoughts, I want to question whether the mind knows only what it senses, or whether the mind senses only what it believes? Do we know only what we think, or do we think only what we believe? Do we know only what we feel, or do we feel only what we believe we feel? Rowe refers to the old saying, '*if I hadn't seen it, I wouldn't have believed it*', as correct in particular circumstances, but in general the saying might better be understood as: '*if I hadn't believed it I wouldn't have seen it*' (Rowe, 2001, p 50). Rowe also notes that '*every meaning contains its opposite because, if the opposite did not exist, no meaning could be created*' (p 51). This is why in this book I introduced complimentary rather than oppositional thinking with the symbol ~ (the notion of complimentary pairs, rather than polar opposites). If we experience what we believe exists, this suggests a need for critical reflexivity about the way that experience is continually constructed and reconstructed: experience is in continual flux and so easily distorted, manipulated, falsified, forgotten, or imagined.

To generate a discussion, create a large rope circle with your students to show the 3Cs, to understand the words of Lao Tzu. The line represents the senses as the primary site of 'Consciousness'. Inside the circle the space represents the internal self, and this operates largely in a 'subconscious', 'Conditioned' way. Outside the circle (the outside world) represents our 'Conduct', our behaviour (see Beard, 2023).

Developing a greater student consciousness is a big ask for teachers: but it is possible. The question then is how do we encourage students to think about their thinking, to sense their sensing, to feel their feelings, and to be conscious of what they are doing and how and why they are doing what they are doing during learning in university? Whilst there has been a relatively recent focus on emotional intelligence, there is more that needs to be understood, including the way our other human capacities for learning can also support mental health and well-being through learning in Higher Education.

Whilst academic content is important, so too is a deeper understanding of the processes by which students experience their learning. Study skills books (e.g. Cottrell, 2024) can help to create an awareness of learning how to learn at an introductory level; beyond this lies a deeper level of attunement, of being consciously aware: '*In learning to live with less self-awareness, we also diminish those distinctively human possibilities for freedom, creativity, caring, and ethical insight which are based on that awareness*' (Cell, 1984, p 9).

The previous quotation is in a chapter called 'Learning and the struggle to be'. Cell then adds:

*Learning to have the power to create power for ourselves exacts a price. It asks us to learn to live with insecurity and anxiety, and this requires courage. To become autonomous and creative, in other words, we need to be in touch with sources of courage.*

(p 9)

Prioritising external validation from parental or authority figures over self-awareness creates the conditions for objective, right, or wrong dualist thinking that offers a reduction in the anxieties that arise from the messy complexity and relativism of life. Light and Cox suggest that this change requires *'a restructuring at an emotional level as well as a cognitive level'* (Light and Cox, 2001, p 57).

# Critical issues

## Exercising power

When teachers fully exercise the power that resides in them there is potential to create dependency. When I introduced the strapline 'Let the Learners Experience the Learning' at a staff development day, one participant asked me whether I was, in fact, still in control! This was astute. I was still in control, but hopefully in a light-touch facilitative sense, to steer and guide our outline agenda, to develop interdependency. Right from the start of these development days, when people ask me how I would like the room set-out, I always say leave it as it is, as this will be our space, not mine!

Good lecturers don't feed students too much content or facts (fish). They feed students just enough to leave them hungry for more, leaving space to teach students to *self*-discover (teaching them to fish), and then they handover the tools for learning (fishing rods, nets … and the bait!). This final stage, in my view, is foundational to experiential learning. This detachment from dependency towards interdependence is important for the transformation of the student becoming and being and it can be carefully crafted through learning design. The ability to purposefully pay attention and become attuned to the unconscious self is not easy, though several practical examples have been highlighted throughout this book. These processes can start right from the beginning of the student studies, in week one. An 'introduction' design was outlined earlier in chapter 3 (Example 3.1) to show how groups of new students can be asked to construct carefully crafted questions to ask in ways that help students to start to take responsibility for their learning in the first few days of their studies. This approach can be frontloaded, by me saying, tongue in cheek: if you ask boring questions, you will get boring answers!

# Increasing consciousness, awareness, and noticing (u - CAN)

The idea of student 'belonging' has been gaining interest in Higher Education over the last ten years or so, and now the student 'being' is attracting a renewed interest, particularly regarding the development of a consciousness of the whole self. This consciousness requires the learner to move between being an experiential 'actor' to that of an experiential 'observer' of the self. Clinical psychologist Siegel (2007) outlines the importance of an integrated and coherent self, in a whole-person sense, noting that learning can contribute towards this notion of balance which underpins health and well-being.

Whilst Higher Education has for a long time played an important role in developing the student sense of becoming and being in the world, there is more to do. By pulling together many of the design principles presented in this book, experiential designs offer many possibilities for a heightened consciousness in relation to the student conduct and conditioning. Together the six chapters show how design can increase the conscious experiencing of belonging, doing, acting, feeling, and thinking during student learning. Holistic designs that combine the experience *'for'* and *'of'* learning have considerable potential to bring about balance, integration, and coherence in the student self, and this can be transformative. For example, experiencing purpose, being productive, thinking differently, and gaining pleasure from learning can all be made more visible to students through intentional experience design.

## Example 6.2

### Practical examples of increased awareness

Two important straplines are: (1) 'Let the Learners Experience the Learning' and (2) 'Make the Experience of Learning Visible'. Consciously experiencing the processes of learning exposes the capacities that students possess, bringing about a process of noticing, of making the whole experience more visible. Learning design examples could include, for example:

1. Asking questions to enhance noticing. A basic example might be: tell me what you are thinking, tell me what you can see, tell me what you have noticed in terms of the role that your hands play in the manipulation of these practical objects to expose patterns and relationships that are in turn leading you to develop a conceptual understanding. Asking students to talk about what they

can see, or observe, at a simple descriptive level starts a process that eventually, with encouragement, develops into higher levels of consciousness.

2. Develop group *self*-review cards: rather than lead a review, design *self*-reviews, *self*-guidance, and *self*-reflection cards for student groups to use to start to develop their own ability to understand the role of self-*review*, self-*reflect*, self-*revisit*, self-*recollect*, self-*reconsider*, self-*rewrite*, self-*rethink*, self-*recraft*, and self-*remembering*, for example.

3. Use Learning Route Maps to support students by showing the journey of where module learning is now, where it has been, and what it is leading towards. If these route maps can be made digital, and located on student smart phones, then such maps can be used to encourage the students to *self*-monitor and *self*-navigate their journey more often.

4. Develop conscious raising codes like H.D.O.A.C, as used in the Industrial Ecology example. This code guides the actions of students as the experience unfolds, encouraging a shift from object manipulation to conceptual thought. This process raises the consciousness of the stages and range of capacities utilised in the move towards higher levels of critical, creative, and conceptual thinking.

5. Use 'Live' Crafting methods. This is a lecturer-student co-creative writing process that makes conscious the creative, yet messy iterative processes involved in writing (e.g. crafting a summary). This involves using speech technology to develop writing live *on-screen* by lecturers who are willing to both encourage students to contribute, whilst at the same time joining in the process and making visible their own abilities and difficulties to craft good writing. For students I have found this experience can be more powerful than asking them to read study skills books.

6. Create Memory Enhancement processes: increasing awareness of the role of the movement of the body, alongside spatial cognition in ways that enhance memory. This experience involves the production of a booklet. The process involves walking through a large version of the learning route maps created on the floor by student teams to develop their own commentaries about their learning for each weekly seminar or lecture, in terms of (1) what they did or experienced and (2) what they learned from what they did. These commentaries are then easily turned into student generated memory booklets using speech recognition. I often offer to create the draft booklet they designed and promise to send it out the next day.

7. Create and make visible steps or stages (e.g. of Customer Service Recovery). I use a real critical incident that occurred in Business Class on Lufthansa Airlines for student groups to discuss and then create a solution-focused Customer Service Recovery approach using no more than four to six stages, sequences, or steps. I sometimes play this experience out, pretending to be an

airline steward and students are often hurting with laughter! I stop at a critical point and then, as the tutor, I ask: Walk me through your solution, your steps to customer recovery. Comparison between groups allows for further awareness raising, which generates discussion about common understanding and differences as a social interaction process that can deepen the sense of belonging.

8. Explore impulses: such as Addictive Behaviour Awareness and the sequence (known by many businesses) that intentionally creates triggers, then habits and then addictions. For example, Awareness of Social Media Addictive Behaviours by raising awareness of, for example, screen time presented in the development of time management skills.

9. Create Awareness of the need to belong, and the deep human need for (1) affiliation in terms of friendships and secure attachments (endorphins create a positive, calming emotional affect) including the need for (2) achievement (dopamine creates a positive emotion as a buzz, or high) (see Beard et al., 2007).

10. Create Awareness of the Four Life Positions of the OK Corral, and the way that the three Ps contribute to Happiness: Pleasure, Purpose, and being Productive in life. Introduce students to the deep learning that occurs by understanding these issues about the self.

11. Ask students to discuss their positive feelings of pleasure that arise from their learning. Do students ever get a platform in classes to speak about their pleasures of learning (for three papers on the pleasure of learning see Beard et al., 2007; Humberstone et al., 2013; Beard et al., 2014)? The reading experience in chapter 4 is an example that encourages awareness of the pleasure of reading.

# Developing integration and balance through experience design

Figure 6.1 is a simple visual representation of the HELT. A circle is used to represent a wheel as a visual metaphor highlighting the need for balance and integration of the seven capacities that humans utilise to experience the world.

Integration and balance are the subject of international initiatives to identify the 21st century competences that should be developed and embedded within a range of educational systems. Underpinning these initiatives is a liberatory desire to create a more democratic society, with new global thinking about ways of being. The United Nations Human Development Index, for example, is a measure of well-being that embraces three interlinked areas: health, education, and living standards. Competency discussions have centred on the expansion of people's freedoms to live long, healthy lives, and to actively engage in shaping the equitable and sustainable future of a shared

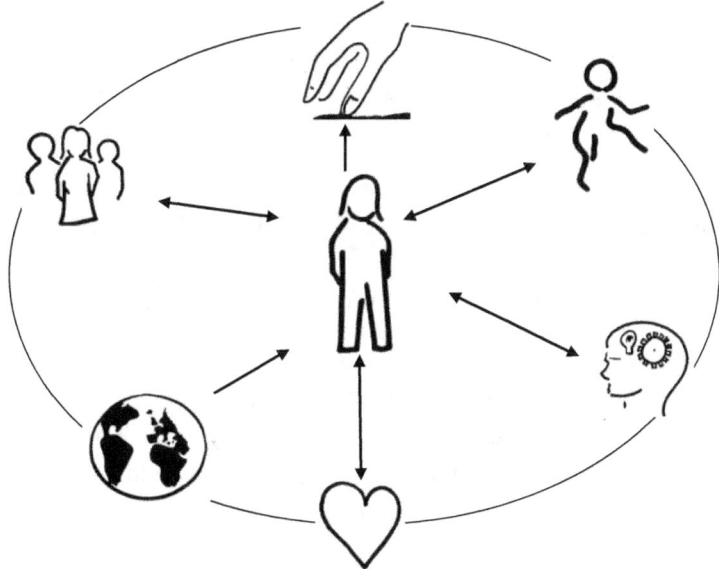

**Figure 6.1** Balance and integration in the Holistic Experiential Learning Theory (HELT) model

planet. In 2018 the Council of the European Union recommended that key competences be established for lifelong learning, to support change and adaptation so that people could achieve personal fulfilment and satisfaction, develop themselves and relate to others, and learn how to learn, and be employable. These skills are said to be essential for social inclusion and for civic participation in society, to enable people to cope with complexity, be thriving individuals, responsible social agents, and become reflective lifelong learners.

The European Union has created nine competences that are important for everyone within formal, informal, and non-formal education. They are structured into three intertwined competence areas that relate to integration of Personal, Social, and Learning to Learn capacities. Personal relates to self-regulation (awareness and management of emotions, thoughts, and behaviour), flexibility (ability to manage transitions and uncertainty, and to face challenges), well-being (pursuit of life satisfaction; care of physical, mental and social health; and adoption of a sustainable lifestyle). Social relates to the development of empathy (the understanding of another person's emotions, experiences, and values, and the provision of appropriate responses), communication (use of relevant communication strategies, domain specific codes, and tools, depending on the context and the content), collaboration (engagement in group activity and teamwork acknowledging and respecting others). Learning to Learn relates to the growth of the self, with a mindset that creates belief in one's and others' potential to continuously learn and progress; critical thinking (assessment of information and arguments to support reasoned conclusions and develop innovative solutions); and the management of learning (the planning, organising, monitoring, and reviewing of one's own learning).

The Singapore Ministry of Education observed an alignment of their emerging 21st century Competences with the HELT. In 2015, to support their embedding of competency initiatives into schools, I was asked to merge the model to form a simple overview, and to design and deliver workshops for Singaporean teachers.

Singapore developed student socio-emotional competences, including self-awareness, self-management, responsible decision-making, social awareness and relational management. These are seen as the skills that are necessary for school pupils to develop healthy identities; recognise and manage their emotions; develop a sense of responsibility, care, and concern for others; relate to others and develop positive relationships; handle challenges; make responsible decisions; and act for the good of self, others, and society. The Singapore Ministry of Education also developed an additional set of significant core values. Their core values include respect, responsibility, resilience, integrity, care, and harmony, and these are acknowledged as values that are foundational to their shared societal and national values.

## Example 6.3

### Monitoring of the student learning experience

As an Educational Excellence Board Member of a major apprenticeship company, I introduced the use of the HELT to better understand learner experiences. The company now collects detailed data as 'indicators of excellence' using six of the capacities for learning. For the feeling (affective) dimension, the organisation is exploring how 'this capacity addresses the emotional and psychological aspects of learning, focusing on how learners feel throughout the process'. Illustrative feedback data explores questions about whether:

- Learners express feeling supported, motivated, and confident during the course.
- Learners report a sense of well-being and personal growth throughout the learning process.
- Emotional challenges such as frustration or stress are acknowledged and managed constructively.

Illustrative feedback indicators on Belonging currently consider whether:

- Learners feel included, respected, and valued within their learning community.
- Learners experience positive relationships with peers, mentors, and instructors.
- Learners express a strong sense of community and collaboration in the learning environment.

Other comprehensive key indicators of excellence continue to evolve.

# Belonging in the More Than Human World (MTHW)

In his book titled *Sustainable Education: Re-visioning Learning and Change*, Sterling (2001, p 75) notes that *'in 1996 an international commission report to UNESCO proposed four pillars as the foundations of education. These are in sum: learning to live together, learning to know, learning to do, and learning to be'*. *Oikos* is a Greek word, referring to household or living place, and it is the basis of the word ecology (coined by Ernst Haeckel in 1873). Place, home, and ecology are all connected to the human sense of belonging.

Kadoorie Farm and Botanic Gardens (KFBG) is a remarkable organisation located in a special place known as *The Garden in the Sky* that has been the subject of a set of films narrated by Sir David Attenborough. Their mission, vision, and core values create further contextual understanding for the proposals in this chapter. The KFBG *mission* is to harmonise the human relationship with the environment. Their Vision is a world in which people live sustainably with respect for each other and nature. Their Core Values present more detail about their underlying approach to ways of working and being in the world.

Having worked with KFBG for many years on the slopes of the mountain forest, it is noticeable how the natural surroundings create positive conditions for learning. It has become clear to me that this organisation gave much thought to the creation of the values that underpin everything they do. An exploration of just three of their seven value statements will highlight their distinctive approach: (1) *Sustainable Living*: Appreciating the impact of our actions with regard to current and future generations: Having awareness of our connection with the environment: Valuing simple and responsible lifestyles. (2) *Love*: Having self-awareness and understanding of the inter-relationship of all things: Having compassion and respect for all life: Recognising that outer discord is a reflection of inner discord. Striving for inner silence. (3) *Happiness*: Appreciating that our happiness lies in creating and sharing happiness with others. Returning to the core value of LOVE, ask yourself if you have ever heard or seen any organisation promote these values.

Finally, two lecturers in Hong Kong spontaneously created a dance as they walked through the HELT model. They called it the 'ing' dance (be-*ing*, do-*ing*, etc.). This dance was an improvisation and came into being as a complex ever-changing flux involving all the humans experiencing capacities. I mention this improvisation as this kind of spontaneity surfaces continually in our teaching: the experience unfolds, and not everything can be designed, predicted, or even languaged. This experience also created much laughter amongst participants: but why is this important? As Nord (2023, p 21), from her work at the Mental Health Neuroscience Lab at Cambridge University, notes, '*one example of the simple things that evoke natural opioids release is laughing with friends*.' Research on the pleasure of learning and positive emotions (Beard et al., 2007; Beard et al., 2014) shows how the pleasure of learning is often neglected, yet pleasure is at the heart of good mental health.

## Summary

- Experiential learning design is certainly not easy. It takes time and patience to develop the necessary skills to create experiences of and for learning, and as an iterative process it ideally should involve a team of designers. Good design requires several returns to the drawing board over time to craft both the science of lesson planning and objective setting with the artistic choreographic design processes. More complex levels of design can result in an increase in consciousness, awareness, and noticing (C.A.N) of the core capacities that are variably harnessed in order to learn in ways that can be transformative.

- New experiential design ideas are being embedded within and related to the competences that are regarded as important for the 21st century. Interestingly, competences are being developed to create more democratic societies. Once again, a liberatory element surfaces in this educational design thinking. The HELT design modelling is also being used to collect data and to monitor excellence in the design and provision of learning experiences.

# Useful texts

Siegel, D (2007) *The Mindful Brain: Reflection and Attunement in the Cultivation of Well-being*. New York: Norton.

*The book explores the development of an integrated and balanced self in the cultivation of well-being. The book includes a detailed exploration of the ontogenetic and phylogenetic development of the mind.*

Baxter Magolda, M (2011) Authoring your life: a lifewide learning perspective, in Jackson, N (ed.) *Learning for a Complex World: A Lifewide Concept of Learning: Education and Personal Development*, pp 76–99. Bloomington, IN: Author-House.

*Learning inside the university is not disconnected to learning outside the university. This chapter explores the notion of 'authoring' one's own life in a book about the less well-known idea or concept of lifewide as opposed to lifelong learning.*

## Chapter 7 | Final thoughts

In Higher Education the need to embrace diversity and inclusivity remains important, yet many of the capacities for learning available to students are neglected. Learning is no longer focused solely on knowledge and its transmission. In experiential learning the focus is on the design of the student learning 'experience': the word experience is significant because how humans experience the world has direct correspondence with how humans learn. This book argues that in order to understand how students learn, a wider body of multi-disciplinary research should be embraced. Few teachers are exposed to such disciplinary complexity in their training. With a new focus on the experience of learning, the gap between work and learning, and the gap between learning and assessment, can be collapsed: learning, as opposed to knowledge acquisition, is made visible. Learning should be also understood as connected to, embedded in, and influencing a complex lifewide and lifelong experiential ecology that consists of community, corporates, NGOs, public bodies, and governments, within a human socio-cultural, and other-than-human natural and material world.

Early in the book the well-honed human capacities to learn are uncovered in the story of our 'natural history', a story that shows how learning involves much more than the thinking capacities of the brain. The body, for example, and especially the hands, are powerful in their capacity to support student learning. Much of the recent published history of experiential learning is controversial, as it has been influenced by the popularity of specific narratives. Simplistic models of experiential learning, whilst easy to remember and grasp, have, to an extent, spread the idea of experiential learning whilst at the same time limiting its development. Learning design requires an understanding of the core capacities that students utilise for learning, though this is not an easy task. If the complexity of learning continues to be disregarded, inclusivity will remain neglected, and learning will be impoverished. A more comprehensive understanding of experiential learning design is required, and so this book introduces a new Holistic Experiential Learning Theory (HELT) that, whilst embedded in complexity, exhibits a simplicity that embraces both the art and science of experiential learning design.

This book explores a wide range of practical design principles. They are underpinned by research into several of the most significant core capacities that students can utilise for learning. These capacities occur within the embodied, inner, private world of students, with complex sensory capacities connecting this inner world to the outer, embedded world. The outer world experiences include doing and producing things, interacting not only with people, but also a more-than-human world. Together these two worlds constitute the foundational complexity of the student learning experience.

Learning capacities operate in an interconnected way in a constant flux: when in balance these capacities function to create homeostasis, and flourishing. The inner, embodied world capacities include the student feelings (affective), cognition (thinking), and the capacity of being and becoming someone. They all affect student health and their well-being. By increasing the student consciousness, awareness, and noticing (C.A.N) of their experiencing capacities, the ability of students to take control of their mind becomes critical. Much of what happens during learning occurs in subconscious processes, and awareness raising is important in a time when businesses vies for their attention: we live in an 'attention economy'. The brain has a physical genetic template, but it is sculpted by experience, in a process often referred to as plasticity of the mind-brain dynamic.

The chapter on a brief history of experiential learning highlights numerous liberatory intentions about the need for change. Making changes to the way we 'teach' is often difficult, but change should be experienced as potentially liberatory for both staff and students. Change is usually best considered as a long-term endeavour. Teachers often ask my opinion on their perceived concern that students expect to be 'taught', as that is what they are paying for. I have worked across the globe with nearly a hundred Higher and Further Education Institutions, with medical and clinical educators, with businesses, with government departments including supporting the training and development of diplomats and ambassadors in the USA, with the Ministry of Education in Singapore on teacher development, with many UK school teachers, community development groups, and voluntary sector organisations. My answer to all these educators and trainers is always the same: 'if what you are doing is working well, then don't try to fix it'.

Change requires a balanced approach, and there is nothing wrong with a good lecture, for example. Whilst we as lecturers need to use our experience to teach, my view is that teaching is more effective when we use a light touch, as an 'experiential guide'. Let the students experience their learning, most of, but not all, the time.

Enjoy the change process, focus more on experience design, and see what happens, but be patient.

# References

Allman, J (2000) *Evolving Brains*. New York: Scientific American Library.

Barnett, R (2007) *A Will To Learn: Being a Student in an Age of Uncertainty*. Maidenhead: Society for Research into Higher Education and Open University Press.

Barnett, R (2009) Knowing and becoming in the higher education curriculum. *Studies in Higher Education*, 34(4): 429–440.

Barnett, R (2018) *The Ecological University: A Feasible Utopia*. London: Routledge.

Baumeister, R (2011) Self and identity: a brief overview of what they are, what they do, and how they work. *Annals of the New York Academy of Sciences*, 1: 48–55.

Baumeister, R (2022) *The Self Explained: Why and How We Become Who We Are*. London: Guildford Press.

Baumeister, R, Bratslavsky, E, Finkenauer, C and Vohs, K (2001) Bad is stronger than good. *Review of General Psychology*, 5(4): 323–370.

Baumeister, R and Leary, M (1995) The need to belong: desire for interpersonal attachments as a fundamental human motivation. *Psychological Bulletin*, 117(3): 497.

Baxter Magolda, M (2011) Authoring your life: a lifewide learning perspective, in Jackson, N (ed.) *Learning for a Complex World: A Lifewide Concept of Learning: Education and Personal Development*, pp 76–99. Bloomington, IN: Author-House.

Beard, C (2018) Learning Experience Designs (LEDs) in an age of complexity: time to replace the lightbulb. *Reflective Practice*, 19(6): 736–748.

Beard, C (2023) *Experiential Learning Design: Theoretical Foundations and Effective Principles*. New York: Routledge.

Beard, C, Clegg, S and Smith, K (2007) Acknowledging the affective in Higher Education. *British Educational Research Journal*, 33: 235–252.

Beard, C, Humberstone, B, and Clayton, B (2014) Positive emotions: passionate scholarship and student transformation. *Teaching in Higher Education*, 19(6): 630–643.

Beard, C and Wilson, J (2002) Still building rafts, juggling balls and driving tanks? *Horizons*. The Institute for Outdoor Learning, Autumn, 19: 11–19.

Beard, C and Wilson, J (2005) Ingredients for effective experiential learning: the learning combination lock, in Hartley, P, Woods, A and Pill, M (eds) *Enhancing Teaching in Higher Education: New Approaches To Improving Student Learning*, pp 3–15. York: Higher Education Academy.

Beard, C and Wilson, P (2018) (4th edition) *Experiential Learning: A Practical Guide for Training, Coaching and Education*. London: Kogan Page.

Belzer, A and Dashew, B (eds) (2023) *Understanding the Adult Learner: Perspectives and Practices*. Sterling, VA: Stylus Publishing.

Bingham, C and Sidorkin, A (eds) (2004) *No Education Without Relation*. New York: Peter Lang.

Borton, T (1970) *Reach, Touch, Teach*. New York: McGraw-Hill.

Bourg, D and Erkman, S (eds) (2003) *Perspectives on Industrial Ecology*. Sheffield: Greenleaf Publishing.

Bovill, C (2020) *Co-creating Learning and Teaching: Towards Relational Pedagogy in Higher Education*. St. Albans: Critical Publishing.

Bowlby, J (1969) *Attachment and Loss*. Vol. 1. London: Hogarth Press.

Boydell, T (1971) *A Guide to the Identification of Training Needs*. London: Chartered Institute of Personnel and Development.

Boydell, T (1976) *Experiential Learning*. Manchester Monographs, Sheffield City Polytechnic.

Butera, C and Aziz-Zadeh, L (2022) Mirror neurons and social implications for the classroom, in Macrine, S and Fugate, J (eds) *Movement Matters: How Embodied Cognition Informs Teaching and Learning*, pp 261–274. Cambridge, MA: MIT Press.

Caine, R, and Caine, G (1994) *Making Connections: Teaching and the Human Brain*. New York: Addison-Wesley.

Cassidy, J (2016) The nature of the child's ties, in Cassidy, J and Shaver, P (eds) *Handbook of Attachment: Theory, Research, and Clinical Applications* (3rd edition), pp 3–24. London: The Guildford Press.

Cell, E (1984) *Learning to Learn from Experience*. Albany: State University of New York Press.

Chatterjee, H and Hannan, L (2016) *Engaging The Senses: Object-based Learning in Higher Education*. Oxon: Routledge.

Clark, A (2011) *Supersizing the Mind: Embodiment, Action, and Cognitive Extension*. Oxford: Oxford University Press.

Clayton, B, Beard, C, Humberstone, B and Wolstenholme, C (2009) The jouissance of learning: evolutionary musings on the pleasures of learning in higher education. *Teaching in Higher Education*, 14(4): 375–386.

Cobb, M (2021) *The Idea of the Brain: A History*. London: Profile Books.

Cottrell, S (2024) *The Study Skills Handbook*. London: Bloomsbury Publishing.

Crosby, A (1995) A critical look: the philosophical foundations of experiential education, in Warren et al. (eds) *The Theory of Experiential Education*, pp 3–32. Dubuque, IA: Kendall Hunt.

Curtis, S (1963) (5th edition) *The History of Education in Britain*. London: University Tutorial Press.

Curtis, S (1967) (7th edition) *The History of Education in Britain*. London: University Tutorial Press.

Dale E (1969) (3rd edition) *Audiovisual Methods in Teaching*. New York: Holt, Rinehart and Winston.

Dashew, B and Gayeski, D (2023) Instructional design, in Belzer, A and Dashew, B (eds) *Understanding The Adult Learner: Perspectives and Practices*, pp 255–274. Sterling, VA: Stylus Publishing.

Davis, B and Sumara, D (1997) Cognition, complexity and teacher education. *Harvard Educational Review*, 67(1): 105–125.

Davis, W (2009) *The Wayfinders: Why Ancient Wisdom Matters in the Modern World*. Toronto: House of Anansi Press.

Denis, M (2018) *Space and Spatial Cognition: A Multi-disciplinary Perspective*. Oxon: Routledge.

Dewey, J (1938) *Experience and Education*. New York: Touchstone.

Dudchenko, P (2010) *Why People Get Lost: The Psychology and Neuroscience of Spatial Cognition*. Oxford: Oxford University Press.

Fenwick, T (2003) *Learning Through Experience: Troubling Orthodoxies and Intersecting Questions*. Malabar, Fl: Krieger Publishing Company.

Finkel, D (2000) *Teaching With Your Mouth Shut*. Portsmouth, NH: Heinemann.

Gale, T and Parker, S (2014) Navigating change: a typology of student transition in Higher Education. *Studies in Higher Education*, 23(4): 54–60.

Gattis, M (2001) (ed.) *Spatial Schemas and Abstract Thought*. Cambridge, MA: MIT Press.

Gilbert, P (2010) *Compassion Focused Therapy*. London: Routledge.

Goldin-Meadow, S (2003) *Hearing Gesture: How our Hands Help Us to Think*. Cambridge: Harvard University Press.

Gravett, K (2024) Authentic assessment as relational pedagogy. *Teaching in Higher Education*: 1–15.

Gray, T and Mitten, D (eds) (2018) *The Palgrave International Handbook of Women and Outdoor Learning*, London: Palgrave Macmillan.

Greenaway, R (1993) *Playback: A Guide to Reviewing Activities*. The Award Scheme Ptd., Duke of Edinburgh's Award and Endeavour, Scotland.

# REFERENCES

Holman, D, Pavlica, K, and Thorpe, R (1997) Rethinking Kolb's theory of experiential learning in management education, *Management Learning*, 28(2): 135–148.

Holmes, J and Slade, A (2018) *Attachment in Therapeutic Practice*. London: Sage.

Humberstone, B, Beard, C and Clayton, B (2013) Performativity and enjoyable learning. *Journal of Further and Higher Education*, 37(2): 280–295.

Illeris, K (2002) *The Three Dimensions of Learning: Contemporary Learning Theory in the Tension Field Between the Cognitive, the Emotional, and the Social*. Malabar, FL: Krieger Publishing.

Itin, C (1999) Reasserting the philosophy of experiential education as a vehicle for change in the 21st century. *The Journal of Experiential Education*, 22(2): 91–98.

Jarvis, P (2006) *Towards a Comprehensive Theory of Human Learning*. Oxford: Routledge.

Jay, M (2005) *Songs of Experience: Modern American and European Variations on a Universal Theme*. Berkeley: University of California Press.

Jones, H, Mansi, G, Molesworth, C, Monsey, H and Orpin, H (2023) *Transition into Higher Education*. St. Albans: Critical Publishing.

Kelso, J and Engstrom, D (2006) *The Complimentary Nature*. Cambridge, MA: Bradford Book/MIT Press.

Kirsh, D (2010) Thinking with external representations, *AI and Society*, 25: 441–454.

Knudson, H, Woodworth, R and Bell, C (1973) *Management: An Experiential Approach*, New York: McGraw-Hill.

Kolb, D (1973) On management and the learning process, *Sloan School Working Paper*, Cambridge, MA: MIT Press.

Kolb, D (1984) *Experiential learning: Experience as the Source of Learning and Development*. New York: Prentice-Hall.

Kolb, D and Fry, R (1975) Toward an applied theory of experiential learning, in Cooper, C (ed.) *Theories of Group Processes*, pp 32–57. New York: Wiley and Sons.

Kolb, D, Rubin, I and McIntyre, J (1971) *Organizational Psychology: An Experiential Approach*. New York: Prentice Hall.

Kosslyn, S and Miller, G (2013) *Top Brain Bottom Brain*. New York: Simon and Schuster.

Lakoff, G, and Johnson, M (1999) *Philosophy in the Flesh – The Embodied Mind and its Challenge to Western Thought*. New York: Basic Books.

Lakoff, G and Nunez, R (2000). *Where Mathematics Comes From: How the Embodied Mind Brings Mathematics Into Being*. New York: Basic Books.

Laurillard, D (2012) *Teaching as a Design Science: Building Pedagogical Patterns for Learning and Technology*. New York: Routledge.

Levitin, D (2020) *Successful Aging: A Neuroscientist Explores the Power and Potential of Our Lives*. New York: Penguin.

Lewin, K (1951) *Field Theory as a Social Science: Selected Theoretical Papers* (D. Cartwright, ed.). New York: Harper and Row.

Light, G and Cox, R (2001) *Learning and Teaching in Higher Education: The Reflective Professional*. London: Sage.

Lillard, A (2017) (3rd edition) *Montessori: The Science Behind the Genius*. New York: Oxford University Press.

Lundborg, G (2014) *The Hand and the Brain: From Lucy's Thumb to the Thought Controlled Robotic Hand*. New York: Springer.

Mackh, B (2018) *Higher Education by Design: Best Practices for Curricular Planning and Instruction*. New York: Routledge.

Macrine, S and Fugate, J (2022) *Movement Matters: How Embodied Cognition Informs Teaching and Learning*. Cambridge, MA: MIT Press.

Maguire, E, Gadian, D, Johnsrude, I, Good, C, Ashburner, J, Frackowiak, R, and Frith, C (2000) Navigation-related structural change in the hippocampi of taxi drivers. *Proceedings of the National Academy of Sciences*, 97(8): 4398–4403.

Marton, F and Säljö, R (1976) On qualitative differences in learning. 1 – outcome and process. *British Journal of Educational Psychology*, 46: 4–11.

Mayer, R (2014) (ed.) (2nd edition) *The Cambridge Handbook of Multimedia Learning*. New York: Cambridge University Press.

Mayes, C and Williams, E (2013) *Nurturing the Whole Student: Five Dimensions of Teaching and Learning*. Plymouth: Rowman and Littlefield Education.

McGilchrist, I (2009) (expanded edition) *The Master and His Emissary: The Divided Brain and the Making of the Western World*. New Haven, CT: Yale University Press.

McGilchrist, I (2019) *Ways of Attending*. Oxon: Routledge.

Michelson, E (1998) Re-remembering: the return of the body to experiential learning. *Studies in Continuing Education*, 20(2): 217–233.

Miettinen, R (2000) The concept of experiential learning and John Dewey's theory of reflective thought and action. *International Journal of Lifelong Education*, 19(1): 54–72.

Moon, J (2004) *A Handbook of Reflective and Experiential Learning: Theory and Practice*. London: Routledge/Falmer.

Mortiboys, A (2002) *The Emotionally Intelligent Lecturer*. Birmingham: SEDA Publications.

Nord, C (2023) *The Balanced Brain: The Science of Mental Health*. London: Penguin/Random House.

Palmer, J (ed.) (2001) *Fifty Major Thinkers on Education: From Confucius to Dewey*. London: Routledge.

Parry, J and Allison, P (eds) (2021) *Experiential Learning and Outdoor Education: Traditions of Practice and Philosophical Perspectives*. Oxon: Routledge.

Pine, J and Gilmore, B (1999) *The Experience Economy, Work is Theatre and Every Business is a Stage*. Boston: Harvard Business School.

Pink, D (2010) *Drive: The Surprising Truth About What Motivates Us*. Edinburgh: Canongate Books.

Pounds, W (1965) On problem solving, *Sloan School Working Paper*, pp 145–165. Cambridge, MA: MIT.

Radman, Z (ed.) (2013) *The Hand, An Organ of the Mind: What the Manual Tells the Mental*. Cambridge, MA: MIT Press.

Reed, S (2022) (2nd edition) *Thinking Visually*. New York: Routledge.

Richards, A (1999) Kurt Hahn, in Miles, J C and Priest, S (eds) *Adventure Programming*, pp 65–70. State College, PA: Venture Publishing.

Roberts, J (2012) *Beyond Learning by Doing: Theoretical Currents in Experiential Education*. Oxford: Routledge.

Rowe, D (2001) *Friends and Enemies*. London: HarperCollins.

Sadoski, M, and Paivio, A (2013) (2nd edition) *Imagery and Text: A Dual Coding Theory of Reading and Writing*. New York: Routledge.

Schwetman, J (2014) Harry Beck's London underground map: a convex lens for the global city. *Transfers*, 4(2): 86–103.

Seaman, J (2008) Experience, reflect, critique: the end of the "learning cycles" era. *Journal of Experiential Education*, 31(1): 3–18.

Seaman, J, Quay, J and Brown, M (2017) The evolution of experiential learning: tracing lines of research in the JEE. *Journal of Experiential Education*, 40: 1–20.

Sheets-Johnstone, M (1990) *The Roots of Thinking*. Philadelphia, PA: Temple University Press.

Sheets-Johnstone, M (2009) *The Corporeal Turn, An Interdisciplinary Reader*. Exeter: Imprint Academic.

Sheets-Johnstone, M (2011) (2nd edition) *The Primacy of Movement*. Amsterdam: John Benjamins Publishing Company.

# REFERENCES

Siegel, D (2007) *The Mindful Brain: Reflection and Attunement in the Cultivation of Well-being.* New York: Norton.

Siegel, D (2012) (2nd edition) *The Developing Mind: How Relationships and the Brain Interact to Shape Who We Are*, New York: Guildford Press.

Siegel, D (2015) (2nd edition) *The Developing Mind: How Relationships and the Brain Interact to Shape Who We Are.* New York: The Guildford Press.

Stein, M (2004) Theories of experiential learning and the unconscious, in Gould, L, Stapley, L and Stein, M (eds) *Experiential Learning in Organisations: Applications of the Tavistock Group Relations Approach*, pp 19–36. London: Karnac Books.

Sterling, S (2001) *Sustainable Education: Re-visioning Learning and Change.* Devon: Green Books.

Stibbe, A (2021) *Ecolinguistics: Language, Ecology and the Stories We Live By.* Oxon: Routledge.

Stonehouse, P, Allison, P and Carr, D (2011) Aristotle, Plato, and Socrates: Ancient Greek perspectives on experiential learning, in Smith, T and Knapp, C (eds) *Sourcebook of Experiential Education: Key Thinkers and Their Contributions*, pp 13–25. New York: Routledge.

Swarbrooke, J, Beard, C, Leckie, S and Pomfret, G (2003) *Adventure Tourism: The New Frontier.* London: Butterworth-Heinemann.

Swinderski, M (2011) Maria Montessori: founding mother of experiential education?, in Smith, T and Knapp, C (eds) *Sourcebook of Experiential Education: Key Thinkers and Their Contributions*, pp 197–207. New York: Routledge.

Taylor, H (1991) The systematic training model: corn circles in search of a spaceship. *Management Education and Development*, 22(4): 258–278.

Torbert, W (1972) *Learning from Experience: Towards Consciousness.* New York and London: Columbia University Press.

Van Geert, E and Wagemans, J (2020) Order, complexity, and aesthetic appreciation. *Psychology of Aesthetics, Creativity, and the Arts*, 14(2): 135–154.

Veevers, N and Allison, P (2011) *Kurt Hahn: Inspirational, Visionary, Outdoor and Experiential Educator.* Rotterdam: Sense Publishing.

Verschaffel, L, De Corte, E, De Jong, T and Elen, J (2010) *Use of Representations in Reasoning and Problem Solving: An Overview.* London: Routledge.

Wenger, E (1998) *Communities of Practice: Learning Meaning and Identity.* Cambridge: Cambridge University Press.

Whitton, N (2014) *Digital Games and Learning: Research and Theory.* New York: Routledge.

Wight, A (1970) *Participative Education and the Inevitable Revolution.* Center for Research and Education, Estes Park, Colorado. Retrieved from U.S. Department of Education. Document Resume EA 003 097: 1–44.

Wilcox, A (1999) Reflections on doing, being, and becoming. *Australian Occupational Journal*, 1(46): 1–11.

Zhang, Q and Gee, J (2023) *Sensation, the Intuitive System, and Designed Experience: The Missing Links to Learning for Human Flourishing.* Champaign, IL: Common Ground Research Networks.

# Index

*Note: Italic page numbers refer to figures.*

abstract conceptualisation 55
abstract thinking 55
academic learning, focus 69
academic skills development 62
    support 60
academic staff, teaching process (change) 62
active doing 66–67
active experiential memory enhancement 41
activity trap 47
adaptive processes 14
Addictive Behaviour Awareness 76
addictive behaviours 63
adult learning, approaches 9
adult social action, sensitivity training (usage) 17
adventure education, usage 17
Adventure Tourism 53
affective balance, facilitation 32
affective capacities 7, 42–43
affective exchange 43
affiliation
    capacities 7
    theory 43
agency, relations (exploration) 31
AI-generated answer, usage 51
aliveness, primal sense (generative source) 8
ancient philosophers, contribution 15–16
andragogy 9
animals
    brains, examples 14–15
    type classification 51
animate beings, classifications 51–52
animate forms (lives), kinetic thematic (impact) 49
animation, term (usage) 8
anthropomorphic branding language, prominence 53
anxiety, negative threat emotion (impact) 42
applied academic skills, level 4 teaching (problem) 60–64
argument (cognition), usage 16
Aristotle 15–16
articles/books, repository (staff/student co-construction) 62

attachment, theory 43
attentional focus 6
awareness
    creation 76
    increase 74
    raising 76

balance (development), experience design (usage) 76–78
Beck, Harry 33
becoming, capacities 44–45
behaviouralism 54
Behaviouralism, Cognitivism, Humanism, and Social constructivism, Ecological complexity (B.C.H.S.Ec.) 54–55
being, capacities 44–45
belonging 66–67
    feedback indicators 79
    human need, existence 70
    student need 44
    student sense 62
be-longing/be-ing, linguistic connection 25
*Beyond Learning by Doing: Theoretical Currents in Experiential Education* (Roberts) 23
block teaching 61
bodily metaphors 54–55
body
    brain, co-evolution 14
    role, understanding 40
    usage 7
body-mind partnership 23–24
brain
    anticipation machine 37
    capacity 14–15
    complexity 41
    engagement 32
    functions 6
    integration 45
    negative threat emotions, impact 42
    plasticity, demonstration 39–40
    processing, reduction 33
    sculpting 68
    sensory-motor areas, activation 57

brain (*Continued*)
  unconscious mind control 63
brain-body
  co-evolution 14
  coordination/integration, increase 15
  interaction 40
bringing-into-consciousness 69

cartographic representation, impact 33
change, balanced approach
    requirement 83
chaos, impact 71
choreography 33–35, 48–49, 51
  continuous process, impact 60
  involvement 35
  learning objectives, link 28
  processes, aiding 54
Circular Economy 55
circular models, usage 17
circular thinking models, appearance 19
class (animals/plants) 51
classification 51–52
co-creation 6
  design 11
codes
  complexity, relationship 54–55
  sequence, impact 56–57
co-emergence 24
cognition
  location, axiom (rejection) 24
  scaffolding, metaphors (usage) 38–39
  student thinking capacities 40–41
cognitive apprenticeship 70
cognitive balance, facilitation 32
cognitive navigation, clues (creation) 38
cognitive processing channels 58
cognitive scaffolding 30–31
  spatial metaphors, impact 11
Cognitivism 19, 54
cogs, portrayal 35
collaborative inquiry, occurrence 52
collective drawing board, usage
    (alternative) 61
colour-coded laminated cards 66
commercialised narratives 52–53
communication 61
  skills, development 49–51
  strategies 77–78
community groups (laboratory research),
    sensitivity training (usage) 17

competences
  establishment 77
  socio-emotional competences 78
complex designs, shift 35
complexity 60
  design complexity 66–67
  increase, movement (visual
      representation) *39*
  spatial complexity 55
  theories 23
  understanding 26
complex subjects, understanding 11
complex thinking, development 38–39
complimentary pairs, notion 72
conative capacities/agency 6–7
conceptual understanding, development
    74–75
concrete experience 20
  term, usage 10
concrete objects, relational/conceptual
    understanding 31
conditioned self, experience (relationship)
    71–72
confidence, feeling (learner expression) 78
consciousness, awareness, and noticing
    (C.A.N.), increase 83
consciousness, awareness, and noticing
    (u-CAN), increase 74
consciousness, increase 74
consciousness, primary site 72
conscious raising codes, development 75
constituent topic experiences, design 34–35
constructivist orientation 24
container theory 51
content, building 34
continuous assignment support,
    emphasis 62
coordination, brain function 6, 71
co-production, design 11
core design principles, summary *48*
Council of the European Union, competences
    establishment 77
counting, experience 7
creative practice, experiential learning design
    (relationship) 47
critical discourse analysis 52–53
critical incident, example (usage) 75–76
critical thinking 23
customer recovery, steps 76
Customer Service Recovery 75

Dale, Edgar 16
'Death by PowerPoint' 2, 37
   reduction 33–34
deconstruction method 34
deep learning (support), navigational/
   scaffolding aids (usage) 11
deficits, identification (opportunity) 50
demmaterialisation 57
depictive formats 33
depictive icons, usage *34*
descriptive formats 33
descriptive text, usage *34*
design
   complex designs, movement 35
   complexity 66–67
   core design principles, summary *48*
   core student capacities, usage 28
   initiation 28
   level 4 module, design 62–63
   level 7 Walk-the-Talk design 64–66
   linguistics, significance 11
   recognition, absence 64
   redesigning 5–6
   seminar route maps, design *34*
   sequence/shape/flow, involvement 35
   simple designs, movement 35
   start, return 35
   structures *30*
   zone 31
   zone, illustrative contents *32*
design principles 63–64, 82–83
   creation 47–48, *48*
   usage, alternative 61
*Developing Mind: How Relationships and the Brain Interact to Shape Who We Are* (Siegel) 9
Dewey, John 4, 10, 17, 23
   achievement, absence (lament) 21–22
digital games, media types (usage) 58
discovery, scientific method 17
dividing, process 7
doing
   substitution 2
   thinking, non-separation 49
domain specific codes 77–78
Dual Coding Theory 58
Duke of Edinburgh Award 17

eco-linguistics 52
   analysis 53

ecological context 52
eco-tourism 52
   narratives, analysis 53
education
   experiential inclusiveness 1
   outdoor/adventure/nature education, usage 17
educational efficiencies, introduction 21
Educational Excellence Board meeting, attendance 61
Education University of Hong Kong, staff development event design 33
embodied cognition 40
embodied learning 40
emotional challenges, acknowledgement/
   management 78
emotional climate, shaping 42
*Emotionally Intelligent Lecturer, The* (Mortiboys) 42
emotions, brain function 6, 14, 71
enacted learning 3
end zone 32
   designs, concentration 35
   initiation, objectives (usage) 34
enquiry, focus 45
environmental awareness, need 17
environmental movement evolution (co-construction) 65
errors of imagination 37–38
   reduction 38, 53–55, 57
European Union, competences 77–78
'Evolution of the UK Environmental Movement, The' (topic example) 64–65
Ewald, Marina 22
experience
   conditioned self, relationship 71–72
   core elements 69
   economy, experiential learning (term, usage) 9
   impact 4
   learning, human capacities 14
   navigation 33
   philosophy 4
   zone experiences, design 31–32
*Experience and Education* (Dewey) 4, 5
experience design 55
   usage 76–78
experience, harnessing 11
experience-reflect-learn constructivist theory 23

# INDEX

experiential education, definition 10
experiential field trips, providing 62
Experiential Institute, The 22
experiential learning 68
   20th century developments 16–18
   21st century 22
   comprehension, improvement 15–16
   cycle 18
   defining, attempts 10–11
   development 1
   ecological complexity 36–37
   holistic trajectory 22
   idea, spread 82
   liberatory intentions 21
   popularity, increase 8–10
   prejudice 21
   processes, observation 5
   roots 13
   term, search 20
   theoretical position 8
experiential learning design 1, 40–41
   complexity 60
   creative practice, relationship 47
*Experiential Learning Design: Theoretical Foundations and Effective Principles* (Beard) 3, 24
experiential learning history 13
   contextual settings, understanding 19–21
Experiential Learning Model 19
extended learning 3
exterior sensory capacities (exteroceptors), engagement 47
external world experiences 47
extraneous load, reduction 33

family (animals/plants) 51
fear, negative threat emotion (impact) 42
feedback
   data 78
   defining 50
   development 49–51
   indicators 79
   information sources 50
   loops 18
   ongoing practice 51
   skills, development 49–50
   student definitions, live recordings 49
feelings, evocation 50
Fenwick, Tara 23
financial investment, increase 62

first-hand experience, gaining 55
five-zone design *30*
five-zone map, drawing 34
flux, state 26
forgetfulness 4
foundational capacities 36–37
freedom, expansion 76–77
frustration, acknowledgement/management 78
Further Education 54
Further Education Institution 83

*Garden in the Sky, The* 79
genera (animals/plants) 51
gesture-touch, addition 58
Gordonstoun School 17
graphic design 33–35
group self-review cards, development 75

habits, embedding 71
Haeckel, Ernst 79
Hahn, Kurt 17, 22
handle, discuss, organise, analyse, conceptualise (H.D.O.A.C.)
   code, usage 55
   conscious raising codes, development 75
   guiding code, creation 56
hands
   manipulation 40
   usage 55
happiness, result 42–43
Happiness, value statement 80
haptic interface, evolution 58
haptics, importance 40
*her*-story 21–22
Heuristic Method 17
Heuristics 16
hexagon image, usage 39
Higher Education
   concern 10
   learning 11, 37
   self, transformation 70
   text, reading/unpacking 54–55
*Higher Education by Design: Best Practices for Curricular Planning and Instruction* (Mackh) 3
Higher Education Institutions (HEIs), experiential learning specialists (role) 8
higher-level executive functions, capability 15
hippocampus, enlargement 4, 14–15

*his*-tory 21–22
*History of Education in Great Britain, The* (Curtis) 21
holistic experiential learning
  model (21st century) 24–26
  theory *25*
Holistic Experiential Learning Theory (HELT) 1, 82
  adaptation 22
  balance, usage *77*
  creation/introduction 4, 24–25
  dimensions, alignment 70
  emerging 21st century Competences, alignment 78
  focus 69
  integration, usage *77*
  model, usage 80
  potential 68
  proposal 44
  resonance 70
  usage 78
  visual representation 76
holistic learning models, arguments 35
holistic philosophy 10
*How Relationships and the Brain Interact to Shape Who We Are* (Siegel) 35
human capacities, impact 44–45
human developmental life, kinetic thematic (impact) 49
human energy powered torch, usage 57
Humanism 54
human learning
  capacities, pre-history/development 14
  complexity, acknowledgement (failure) 37
  literature, multi-disciplinary body 35
  research 3
human possibilities, diminishment 72
human relations, sensitivity training (usage) 17
human sensory capacities, improvements 15
human spatial awareness, insight 39–40

Icon, movement 62
ideas/answers, generation 50
Illeris, Knud 35
illustrative contents *32*
images
  conjuring 38
  student reading/analysis 52

imagination
  cognitive processing, complexity 38
  errors, reduction 53–55, 57
implied judgement, involvement 50
improvisational dance, kinetic thematic (impact) 49
impulses, exploration 76
inbound information, passage 37
inclusive learning design 35
inclusive pedagogies 7
inclusivity
  embracing, designs (impact) 11
  neglect 82
Industrial Ecology (IE)
  example, H.D.O.A.C. code (usage) 75
Industrial Ecology (IE), concept 56–57
industrial food chain 56
industrial systems, mimicry 56
industrial wastes, systematic recovery 56
infant hands, dexterity (importance) 7
inferred judgement, involvement 50
Informational Phase 65
Information Phase 65
'ing' dance 80
inheritance, design 11
inner world
  engagement 11
  outer world, relationship 26
instructional methods 69
integration (development), experience design (usage) 76–78
intentional experience design 74
interest, nodal clusters 39
internal world experiences 47
interpersonal interaction, brain function 6, 14, 71
interrelated issues, revealing 39
intersectionality 39

Jarvis, Peter 36
Jay, Martin 8–9
judgement, involvement 50

Kadoorie Farm and Botanic Garden (KFBG), location 79
kinasthesia, omission 39
kinetic thematic, impact 49
kingdom (animals/plants) 51
knowledge

knowledge (*Continued*)
  dissemination 69
  transmission 2
Kolb, David 17

laboratory research, sensitivity training (usage) 17
language
  brain function 6, 14
  communication tool 53–54
*La Novelle Femme* (film) 22
Lao Tzu 71–72
learners
  inner world, engagement 11
  support/motivation/confidence, expression 78
learning
  academic learning, focus 69
  combination lock 36
  core student capacities, design usage 28
  cycles, emergence 17
  embodied learning 40
  experiential learning 1, 8–10
  experiential learning, defining (attempts) 10–11
  focus 9
  foundational student capacities, introduction 37–41
  foundation, experience (harnessing) 11
  human capacities, pre-history/development 14
  inclusive learning design 35
  journey 29
  learner action 1–2, 29–30
  learner experience 29–30, 62, 74
  management 78
  materials, student co-creation 64
  movement, importance (reason) 8
  multi-disciplinary/holistic design approaches 6
  multiple student learning capacities, harnessing 35
  objectives, choreography (link) 28
  objectives-outcomes, writing 29
  processes, combination 36
  products 5
  purpose 4
  spatial cognition, importance (reason) 8
  student learning, experience (improvement) 11–12
  student learning, pedagogically inclusive designs (impact) 6–7
  student pleasure, positive feelings (discussion) 76
  visibility, making (approach) 31, 74
  visibility, making (concept) 11
'learning by doing' 1–2, 36
learning capacities *25*, 78
  harnessing 50
  operation 83
learning design
  architect role 3
  choreographic processes 49
  process (choreography) 48
learning experience 30
  change, academic critiques/calls 23–24
  meaning 3–5
  sequence/flow, re-checking 35
  understanding, multi-disciplinary perspective (usage) 23
  visibility, making 74
Learning Experience Design (LED) 66–67
  complexity, embracing (21st century) 36–37
  two-fold approach 47
  usage 68
Learning Process (reflective questioning approach) 20
Learning Route Maps
  development *30*
  usage 41, 62, 75
*Learning to Learn from Experience* (Bell) 68
learn-to-learn ability 68
lecture material (online posting), PDF file (usage) 63
lecturer-student co-creative writing process 75
level 4 module, design 62–63
level 4 teaching, problem 60–64
level 7 design 60
level 7 Walk-the-Talk design 64–66
Lewin, Kurt 9, 18
liberating structures 29
liberatory intentions 21
linguistic metaphors 29
linguistics, significance 11
live crafting methods, usage 75
live experience (attention), incentives (emphasis) 63

live on-screen writing (development) speech technology (usage) 75
locomotive function 15
logical thinking, usage 16
London Underground
 design 34
 Map 33
 Map, design 65–66
long-term design, vision (student co-creation) 64
long-term learning design, creation 64
long-term relations, initiation 31
Love, value statement 80
Lowe, Robert 21
Lufthansa Airlines critical incident (occurrence/example), student group discussion 75–76

management
 games, usage 10
 learning, focus 18
maps
 communication 29
 populating *30*
marketing promotion 23
mathematics teaching, approaches 7
meanings, selection 38
memory
 enhancement, focus 32
 journey, usage 40
 space, association 4
Memory Enhancement processes, creation 75
mental health
 behaviours 63
 experiences, impact 63
 issues, creation 42
 well-being, connection 11
Mental Health Neuroscience Lab 80
mental video 38
metaphors
 bodily metaphors 54–55
 scaffolding usage 38–39
 spatial metaphors 29, 54
 up-down metaphors 54
'Method of Loci' usage 40
Michelson, Elana 23
middle design zone, topic advancement 32
middle zone (main zone), completion 34–35
mind (self-creation), brain (usage) 71
mind-brain dynamic, plasticity 83

mirror neurons, usage 42
module
 academic staff teaching process, change 62
 design, financial investment increase 62
 guides, usage 29
 iterations 60
 leader, assistance/support 61
 level 4 module, design 62–63
 shape/flow, creation 62
Montessori, Maria 21–22
More Than Human World (MTHW), belonging 79–80
motion, brain function 6, 14, 71
motivation, feeling (learner expression) 78
motor systems, importance 40–41
movement
 brain sections, devotion 15
 importance 14–15
 importance, reason 8
 process 49
moving/sensing, non-separation 49
multi-directional designs, classroom usage 43
multi-disciplinary research, embracing 82
multi-media design principles, usage 33–34
multi-media formats 33
multiple student learning capacities, harnessing 35

narratives
 commercialised narratives 52–53
 dominance 17, 20
natural ecosystems, quasi-cyclical functions (mimicry) 56
nature education, usage 17
nature study, need 17
navigational aids, usage 11
navigational clues 33
navigational support tool 62
negative emotions (counterbalancing), positive emotions (usage) 42
negative threat emotions, impact 42
neural pathways (creation), experiences (impact) 4
neurodiversity 41
 embracing, designs (impact) 11
 term, popularity 5
neuronal processing patterns 41
neurons
 firing 41

neurons (*Continued*)
  mirror neurons, usage 42
  visuomotor neurons, firing 43–44
'New Educational Fellowship' emergence 17
non-integrated self, rigidity (impact) 71
noticing
  enhancement, questions (asking) 74–75
  increase 74
  process 74
*Nurturing the Whole Student: Five Dimensions of Teaching and Learning* (Mayes/Williams) 70

Object Based Learning (OBL) 40
objectives
  deconstruction 34
  development 48
  usage 34
objects, manipulation 55, 74–75
observational skills, requirement 51–52
observations, series (involvement) 50
OK Corral Life Positions
  awareness, creation 76
  Transactional Analysis 63
ontological self, transformation 70
oppositional thinking 5
order (animals/plants) 51
*Organizational Psychology: An Experiential Approach* (Kolb, et al.) 9
other-than-human natural/material world 82
outdoor education, usage 17
outdoor learning 47
outer world/inner world, relationship 26
Outward Bound 17

Parchure, Vishwas 22
Participative approaches 16
Participative Education, term (borrowing) 19
participative pedagogic methods, experiential learning (importance) 19
patterns, exposure 74–75
'Payment by Results' (performance measure) 21
PDF file, usage 63
pedagogically inclusive designs, impact 6–7
pedagogic changes 3
pedagogic design 52
peer relation building 62
People's College 26
perceptual systems, importance 40–41
performance
  calculation 5
  subjective analysis 50
personal growth, learner report 78
personal skills, development (support) 60
phases, creation 65
phygital product, identification 57
phyla (animals/plants) 51
Piaget, Jean 18
plan-do-evaluate cycles 18
'plan, do, review' circular models, popularity (increase) 17
plants, type classification 51
plastic cards, technological capacities 57
Plato 15–16
Pleasure, Purpose, and being Productive (three Ps) 42, 76
points of view 38–39
  representation 39
popularist ideas, appearance 20
positive learning habits (creation), co-production/co-creation/inheritance (design) 11
post-experience reflection 55
power
  exercising 73
  relations, exploration 31
practice, diversification 8
prejudice 21
*Primacy of Movement, The* (Sheets-Johnstone) 3
problems, identification (opportunity) 50
problem-solving cycle, similarities 18
processing (thinking) speeds, increase 15
product bags 57
professional skills, development (support) 60
psychoanalytic theories 23
psychodynamic, term (usage) 70
psychological security, sense 43

racism, exploration 17
realities, learner study 68–69
reasoning, brain function 71
receptive-perceptive attentional capacities 6–7
reciprocity, understanding 26
reconstruction process 50
redesign, description 63–64
Reed, Stephen 53
referencing, academic skills development 62
reflection experience, focus 32
*Reflective Practice* (Beard) 66
relational learning 3

relational management 78
Relational Phase 65
relationships, exposure 74–75
repressive teaching methods, concerns 16
research-informed teaching, lecturer
    delivery 6
resilience
    increase, request 16–17
    initiation 31
restructuring 73
retention, focus 32
route maps
    design, illustration *33*
    usage 75
Rowe, Dorothy 38

SAS style 47
scaffolding aids, usage 11
scenario planning 38
schools
    environmental awareness, need 17
    nature study, need 17
scientific method(s) 16, 18
seeing, vocalization 74–75
self
    choices, making 44
    experiential observer 74
    integrated/coherent self, importance 74
    ontological self, transformation 70
    student sense, development 44–45
    transformation 70
self-awareness 78
    low level 71–72
self-directed learning 9
self-guidance, design 75
self-recollect role (understanding), student
    ability (development) 75
self-reconsider role (understanding), student
    ability (development) 75
self-recraft role (understanding), student
    ability (development) 75
self-reflection cards, review 75
self-reflect role (understanding), student
    ability (development) 75
self-regulation 77–78
self-remembering role (understanding),
    student ability (development) 75
self-rethink role (understanding), student
    ability (development) 75
self-review
    cards, development 75

role (understanding), student ability
    (development) 75
self-reviews, design 75
self-revisit role (understanding), student
    ability (development) 75
self-rewrite role (understanding), student
    ability (development) 75
seminars
    design 62
    route maps, design *34*
sense making process 11
senses, responses 37
sensing 66–67
    moving, non-separation 49
sensitivity, usage 17
sensory-bodily capacities 16
sensory exteroceptors, presence 37
sensory habituation 2
Sheets-Johnstone, Maxine 3
Sheffield Business School 20
Siegel, Daniel 9, 35
signal contamination, reduction 15
silenced voices 21–22
simple design, movement 35
simulations, usage 10
Singapore Ministry of Education 21st century
    Competences/HELT alignment 78
situative theories 23
skin 40
    sensory exteroceptors, presence 37
smart phones, usage 57
social awareness 78
social belonging 43–44
social bonds, initiation 31
social construction process 50
Social constructivism 54
social diseases, concern 17–18
social interactions 16, 43–44
Social Media Addictive Behaviours,
    awareness 76
socio-emotional competences 78
Socrates 15
solution-focused Customer Service Recovery
    approach, student group discussion/
    creation 75–76
space, memory (association) 4
spatial cognition, importance (reason) 8
spatial complexity 55
spatial metaphors 29, 54
    impact 11
spatial patterns 55

spatial understanding, brain function 6, 14, 71
species (animals/plants) 51
speech technology, usage 75
Sperry, Robert 20
Staffordshire Wildlife Trust 64
start zone, content (building) 34
stimulus-response animal ethology studies, reduction 19
straplines 2–3, 74
stress
  acknowledgement/management 78
  negative threat emotion, impact 42
structural/choreographic design principles, impact 11
student learning experience
  design, initiation 28, 34–35
  improvement 11
  monitoring 78–79
student learning, pedagogically inclusive designs (impact) 6–7
students
  beginning/belonging experiences, design (consideration) 34
  brain, anticipation machine 37
  capacities 30–31
  consciousness, awareness, and noticing (C.A.N.), increase 83
  core studies, connectivity (creation) 62
  emotions/feelings (affective capacities) 42–43
  engagement *34*
  foundational student learning capacities, introduction 37–41
  introduction, question 31
  mental health, experiences (impact) 63
  pleasure, positive feelings (discussion) 76
  relationship, consideration 34
  self-discovery 73
  self, student sense (development) 44–45
  support, learning route maps 75
  thinking capacities (cognition) 40–41
  well-being, enhancement 44
  well-being, experiences (impact) 63
student sensing moving body, capacities 37–40
Student Support Services 68
student-tutor, production 53
study skills books, usefulness 72
sub-species (animals/plants) 51

support, feeling (learner expression) 78
surface learning 65
*Sustainable Education: Re-visioning Learning and Change* (Sterling) 79
Sustainable Living (value statement) 79–80
Systematic Training Cycle (circular model) 20
'Systematic Training Model: Corn Circles in Search of a Spaceship' (Taylor) 19
systematic training model, orthodoxy 19

teacher descriptions, support 38
*Teaching as a Design Science: Building Pedagogical Patterns for Learning and Technology* (Laurillard) 3
*Teaching With Your Mouth Shut* (Finkel) 2
teamworking 61
technological capacities 57
technology bag, examples 57
'Tell, Show, and Dio' Instructional Triangle, creation 16
text
  reading, critical discourse analysis 52–53
  reading, practice 54–55
  student reading/analysis 52
  unpacking 54–55
theory of experience, creation 23
thinking 66–67
  abstract thinking 55
  complex thinking, development 38–39
  doing, non-separation 49
  logical thinking, usage 16
  speeds, increase 15
  student thinking capacities (cognition) 40–41
  visibility, making (concept) 11
  vocalization 74–75
thinking brain, capacities 23–24
*Thinking Visually* (Reed) 53
three Cs 72
*Three Dimensions of Learning: Contemporary Learning Theory in the Tension Field Between the Cognitive, the Emotional, and the Social* (Illeris) 35
three-zone design *30*
three-zone map, drawing 34
three-zone structure 29
tick list collections (trophies) 53
tools/materials, range (design) 11
*Top Brain Bottom Brain* (Kosslyn/Miller) 20

topic
  advancement 32
  experiences, design 34–35
touch (sense), haptics (importance) 40
Tourism Sustainable Development Goals 53
*Towards a Comprehensive Theory of Human Learning* (Jarvis) 36
training cycles
  emergence 17
  orthodoxy 19
Transactional Analysis 63
transformation
  creation 70
  initiation 31
Transformation Phase 66
transformative learning 9
*Transition into Higher Education* (Jones) 29, 68
transmission-based teaching methods 11

UK Workers Education Association, commission 64
unconscious self, attention 73
United World colleges 17
up-down metaphors 54

value statements 79–80
vibration capacities, addition 58
vision, brain function 6, 14, 71
visual format, creation 25
visual memory triggers, enhancement *34*
visual metaphor 76
visuomotor neurons, firing 43–44
voice, relations (exploration) 31

Walk-the-Talk design (level 7) 64–66
  experience, recording/capturing/posting 66
well-being 71
  enhancement, learning experience design (usage) 68
  experiences, impact 63
  learner sense, report 78
  mental health, connection 11
*Where Mathematics Comes From: How the Embodied Mind Brings Mathematics Into Being* (Lakoff/Nunez) 40
Whitton, Nicola 58
whole-person learning (embracing), designs (impact) 11
whole-person pedagogic trajectory 22
whole relationship, concentration 35
Wildlife Adventure Tourism 53
wildlife, portrayal 53
words, usage 37–38
word weaving 49–51
work-loading practices, change (need) 61
work-loading systems 28
writing
  academic skills development 62
  development, speech technology (usage) 75

young children, mathematics teaching (approaches) 7
young people, survival ability (concerns) 16–17

zone experience, design 31–32

For Product Safety Concerns and Information please contact our EU representative GPSR@taylorandfrancis.com
Taylor & Francis Verlag GmbH, Kaufingerstraße 24, 80331 München, Germany

www.ingramcontent.com/pod-product-compliance
Lightning Source LLC
Chambersburg PA
CBHW061420300426
44114CB00015B/2002